Life Is A Gold Mine
Can You Dig It?

Dr. John Stanko

E ergreen
P R E S S

The quotation on page 8 is excerpted from the song, "Place In This World." Reprinted by permission of O'Ryan Music, Inc., Age-To-Age Music, Inc., and Careers-BMG Music Publishing.

Scripture taken from the HOLY BIBLE: NEW INTERNATIONAL VERSION. Copyright ©1973, 1978 by the International Bible Society. Used by permission of Zondervan Bible Publishers.

Life Is A Gold Mine by John Stanko
First Edition Copyright ©1995 John Stanko
Revised Edition Copyright ©2001 John Stanko

Published by Evergreen Press
P.O. Box 91011, Mobile, AL 36691
(800) 367-8203
E-mail: EvergreenBooks@aol.com

ISBN 1581690592

Table of Contents

SECTION FIVE
FAITH: "I'm Just an Old Chunk of Coal, But I'm Gonna Be a Diamond Someday"

To my parents, John and Sophia Stanko,
who set an example of love,
discipline, and hard work
that has stayed with me to this day.

INTRODUCTION

"How much better to get wisdom than gold,
to choose understanding rather than silver!"
— Proverbs 16:16.

Life Is a Gold Mine was born during a time of great personal frustration. In 1985 I was administrator and ministry coordinator for a large local church, and I wasn't happy. There was so much to do in the church, and from my viewpoint, not enough people involved. As we would finish a project, someone would invariably approach me and say something like, "I'm sorry I wasn't involved. I felt the Lord prompting me to do something and offer to help, and I like to do what you were doing, but I was afraid and didn't know anyone, so I didn't volunteer."

Without fail, the person had the skills, gifts, and training that we needed. But even after repeated announcements during church services and inquiries to pastors and leaders, people were still uninvolved.

There were others who expressed to me their desire to be in "full-time ministry." Often employed in significant and well-paying secular jobs, they were discouraged that they weren't in any kind of "ministry." Some actually left those positions and today are still wandering, trying to find how they can best serve the Lord.

Richard Nelson Bolles described this dilemma in his book, *What Color Is Your Parachute?*:

> We want some guidance and help in this area, because we want to marry our religious beliefs with our work, rather than leaving the two—our religion and our work—compartmentalized, as two areas of our life which never talk to each other. We want them to talk to each other and uplift each other.[1]

I began asking the Lord, "How can I help people de-compartmentalize their lives? How can I find volunteers? Better yet, how can I help people find out what they are born to do, and help them do it? How can I help them see that 'full-time' ministry is not the only way to serve the Lord? How can I convince them that if they're doing what You have called them to do—and using their gifts in the process—they are serving You?"

During this time, our church had a send-off for a pastoral staff member. As we were praying for this man and his family, a prophetic word came that changed my life. It was an answer to the questions I had been asking and contained the reasons why so few were involved and so many were unfulfilled. It also contained the remedy for the problem I was facing. Here is part of that prophetic message:

In many countries where there is poverty, it is not because there are not resources. In many nations where people go hungry, it is not because the soil is poor. Where they lack industrial development, it is not because there are not minerals in the ground. It is because the people haven't discovered and learned to use what they have. And because the minerals lie in the earth, and the soil—rich as it is—lies dormant, there is poverty abounding in the land. But when someone comes along who knows what to look for and where to find it and how to use it, there are jobs, and there is productivity, and there is wealth. And some sit in their poverty and say it is unfair that we should be poor and others should be rich, but it is not unfair. It is ignorance. It is not knowing what is beneath their feet and what is around them and what is theirs to use.

So it is in the church of the Lord Jesus Christ. In some parts there is great wealth; there is great growth; there is great power. In other parts there is great drought. There is spiritual starvation, and people perish for want of the Word of God; perish for lack of the Spirit of God; perish for lack of edification. They perish and wane away in their spirits. It is not because the resources are not there, because within them, within those very people, within those very congregations, lie great riches, great promises and great wealth. The need is to discover what is there and use it and appropriate it and get it out so that it can become productive.

When I heard this, I almost jumped out of my chair! First, this told me that the resources were out there. The right people for every job were there. The Holy Spirit had gifted and called each one. There was no lack of people, but there was a lack of knowledge about how to find and motivate them to become productive.

The second thing this told me was that someone needed to help discover and channel the human resources in every church. If someone could call forth the people and the deposit of the Holy Spirit in them, then the body of Christ would become stronger and more effective.

And finally, it let me know that each person had a purpose and gifts that were from the Holy Spirit. It was up to the Spirit as to where and how these resources would be fulfilled and used, and not all of them would find their expression in the Church.

From that day, I set out to develop a seminar and write a book to help people become more productive and fulfilled in their life's purpose. I wanted people to know that they were born to do what they were doing. If their purpose was auto mechanics, I wanted them to know they were serving and worshiping God with each engine tune-up.

From there, I wanted to set people on a course of action that would refine and release those resources. It was in my heart to help every man and woman get out of the grandstands and into the game. I wanted to challenge them to dig for the true riches in their life. *Life Is a Gold Mine: Can You Dig It?* was born.

I chose gold and digging as symbols of what I was after for several reasons. The book of Proverbs says, "My [wisdom's] fruit is better than gold, yes, than fine gold and my revenue than choice silver" (Proverbs 8:19 NKJV). In fact, the Bible is full of comparisons of spiritual things to gold. For instance:

The law from your mouth is more precious to me than thousands of pieces of silver and gold (Psalm 119:72).

The ordinances of the Lord are sure and altogether righteous. They are more precious than gold (Psalm 19:9-10).

These have come so that your faith—of greater worth than gold, which perishes even though refined by fire—may be proved genuine (1 Peter 1:7).

Gold is indeed one of the most precious metals known to man. Yet the Word of God, your faith, and the wisdom and understanding that come from knowing your purpose are more valuable than gold. As I researched the mineral gold, I discovered several characteristics that made it the correct focus for what I wanted to teach.

First of all, gold is found alongside many other minerals, and traces of it are even found in sea water. That's how it is with God's mission for our lives. It is often expressed as we carry out some of the more common aspects of life. We can look at ourselves and what we're doing and not see the riches that are buried there. A little digging, however, reveals what is there and begins the recovery process.

Second, once gold ore is mined, the gold is then easily recovered in the refining process. It's the same with our spiritual resources: a little "refining" and we can shine forth like a nugget of pure gold.

Third was something that I already knew: Gold is attractive in color and brightness. When we function in our God-given purpose, with power and creativity, we're also attractive and exciting to be around.

Finally, gold is durable and malleable. It can endure all kinds of treatment and be shaped into many forms. Purpose is like that. Even after the dealings of God and men, you are still able to function in many different kinds of life and ministry situations.

As I've taught this seminar all over the country, I've found most people are hungry, even desperate, to know what their purpose is and how they can fulfill it. Christian recording artist Michael W. Smith recorded a song that became very popular, even on secular stations. The tune was pleasant, but the words are what I believe captured adults and young people alike:

If there are millions down on their knees,
Among the many, can You still hear me?
Hear me asking, "Where do I belong?"
"Is there a vision that I can call my own?"
Looking for a reason, roaming through the night to find
My place in this world, my place in this world.
Not a lot to lean on,
I need Your light to help me find
My place in this world, my place in this world.

The song echoed the cry of many people—perhaps even you. You may have a deep desire to discover why you were born, to find a vision that is your own, and then to fulfill it or die trying. No one wants to lead a wasted life. You want to be like Paul who, at the end of his life, said: "I have finished the race, I have kept the faith" (2 Timothy 4:7). To say that, you must know what the race is so that you can know when you've finished. You must know what the course is if Jesus is ever to say to you, "Well done, good and faithful servant" (Matthew 25:21).

Mining and refining, however, are hard work. With all the above being true, if you're not willing to dig out your gold, you'll have only the potential for riches. The gold is there, but you can die with it still buried in the recesses of your life. Knowing that the gold is there, the question is, "Can you dig it?" I hope this book will help you do just that. As we "dig," I have included some "gold nuggets" from the book of Proverbs for your consideration.

I would be remiss if I didn't mention one book that greatly influenced my life and thinking in the areas of purpose, goals, and time management. *The 7 Habits of Highly Effective People* by Stephen R. Covey is a book that has sold millions of copies since it was released in 1989; it has impacted many people and companies.

Covey popularized many phrases and concepts that have since become commonplace in management discussions and literature. Anyone who read his book came away with such words as "paradigm," "paradigm shift," "P/PC balance," and "proactivity." There were phrases such as "personality and character ethics," "begin with the end in mind," "Quadrant II," "win/win," "synergize," and "sharpen the saw."

Covey encourages the reader to "read with the purpose in

mind of sharing or discussing what you learn with someone else within 48 hours after you learn it."[2] By doing so, Covey believes that "your perspective will be expanded, your understanding deepened, and your motivation to apply the material increased."[3] I took this advice and taught the book as part of a discipleship class in a prison in Daytona Beach, Florida.

That was a wonderful experience as I taught the seven habits from a biblical perspective. The inmates were challenged and, upon completion of the course, embarked on a project to write their own book entitled *The 7 Habits for the Successful Inmate*.

As I taught and discussed Covey's book with others, however, I found that many believers were looking for a different or deeper spiritual emphasis. Covey's Mormon faith is not adequate for some who feel that his own "paradigm" (which Covey defines as a map or model that helps you understand the world you live in) does not properly define some of the spiritual material he presents.

Covey states, "The principles I am referring to are not esoteric, mysterious, or 'religious' ideas."[4] I would maintain, however—and others would probably agree—that his principles are spiritual, if not religious, and should be treated as such. Not to do so leaves one wondering how true effectiveness can be reached in the will of God.

With that in mind, I'll comment on Covey's book as I write. I do this neither as a critic, for Covey has many good things to say, nor as an expert, for Covey's education and experience are far beyond mine. As a disciple and student of the Word, I will simply try to apply my faith to the principles he discussed in order to offer another perspective.

There is one more thing I want to share before I begin. I have been an administrator for as long as I can remember. Playing office was my favorite game as a child, and I love organization, production, and order. I have also had experience in church work for more than 20 years. And so it is my hope that what is presented is not viewed as just another call to become more organized.

Yes, the need for organization and discipline will come through in this book again and again. But this comes from my "pastoral" concern to see people released to do the will of God for their lives. Disorganization and poor time management can undermine their purpose; I want to see everyone improve in those areas so they can be all they were meant to be.

I want you to know the joy I've known as I've functioned in my life's purpose. I want you to preach, teach, pilot a plane, sew a dress, repair brakes, or serve your boss knowing that you're hitting the mark and functioning in what you were born to do. Wouldn't it be wonderful to know that what you do five, six or seven days a week is as much worship as standing in the pew and singing? Those who function in their purpose fulfill Paul's exhortation in Romans 12:1: "Offer your bodies as living sacrifices, holy and pleasing to God—this is your spiritual act of worship."

Bolles wrote in *What Color is Your Parachute?*,

> Every keen observer of human nature will know what I mean when I say that those who have found some sense of Mission have a very special joy, "which no one can take from them." It is wonderful to feel that beyond eating, sleeping, working, having pleasure and it may be marrying, having children, and growing older, you were set here on Earth for some special purpose, and that you can gain some idea of what that purpose is.[5]

Bolles then presents "a scenario for the romantic" of how it is that we come to know or rediscover our purpose:

> We may imagine that before we came to Earth, our souls, our Breath, our Light, stood before the great Creator and volunteered for this Mission. And God and we, together, chose what that Mission would be and what particular gifts would be needed, which he then agreed to give us, after our birth. Thus, our Mission was not a command given peremptorily by an unloving Creator to a reluctant slave without a vote, but was a task jointly designed by us both, in which as fast as the great Creator said, "I wish" our hearts responded, "Oh, yes." As mentioned in an earlier Comment, it may be helpful to think of the condition of our becoming human as that we became amnesiac about any consciousness our soul had before birth—and therefore amnesiac about the nature or manner in which our Mission was designed. Our searching for our Mission now is therefore a searching to recover the memory of

something we ourselves had a part in designing. I am admittedly a hopeless romantic, so of course I like this picture.[6]

I have given you some steps to follow at the end of each section to apply what you've learned as you seek to recover from your amnesia, but I've kept them basic. Too often, books give you exercises to work through that can take months to complete!

My purpose in writing is to see you fulfill your life's mission as you carry out your daily responsibilities as a student, wife, father, employee, supervisor, or minister. As a pastor, I want to equip you so that you can work effectively. As an administrator, I want to help you do things efficiently. It's from those motives that I write, and it's in that spirit that I hope you receive this work. Your life is indeed a gold mine. Now let's get on with the digging.

SECTION ONE

EFFECTIVENESS: Know Where To Stake Your Claim

"He who works his land will have abundant food, but the one who chases fantasies will have his fill of poverty."—Proverbs 28:19

Chapter One
An Overview

Let's start by looking at Acts 6:1-7:

In those days when the number of the disciples was increasing, the Grecian Jews among them complained against the Hebraic Jews because their widows were being overlooked in the daily distribution of food. So the Twelve gathered all the disciples together and said, "It would not be right for us to neglect the ministry of the word of God in order to wait on tables. Brothers, choose seven men from among you who are known to be full of the Spirit and wisdom. We will turn this responsibility over to them, and will give our attention to prayer and the ministry of the word." This proposal pleased the whole group. They chose Stephen, a man full of faith and of the Holy Spirit; also Philip, Procorus, Nicanor, Timon, Parmenas, and Nicolas from Antioch, a convert to Judaism. They presented these men to the apostles, who prayed and laid their hands on them. So the word of God spread. The number of disciples in Jerusalem increased rapidly, and a large number of priests became obedient to the faith.

The Bible never hides the human weaknesses of those who serve the Lord. Here's an account of a serious problem in the church. The Hebrew and Greek believers were fussing at one another. There was an oversight in care that was at least cultural and at worst racial. There was also inefficiency. People were upset, talking, and complaining. It sounds like life in many churches and organizations today.

It's important to study and understand how the apostles handled this problem. Five principles in these verses will form the basis for this book. The first principle is *effectiveness*. Effectiveness is knowing your purpose and functioning in it. *Vine's Dictionary of Old and New Testament Words* defines effectiveness as being "full of power to achieve results." The apostles were well aware of what God wanted them to do. You, too, have a purpose in life that can also be identified. Your success depends on how closely you stick to it.

Verse four contains the second principle, *excellence*. The apostles set a high goal of devoting themselves to prayer and the Word. They probably had goals of how long to pray, what to study, and how they would carry the Gospel to the nations. It's likewise important for you to set high goals for your job, family, ministry, and personal life; you'll learn how to do this in Section Two.

This leads to a third principle, *efficiency*. The apostles realized a great harvest of people because they were efficient in their use of time and resources. They maximized results while committing a minimum of resources to the task.

The fourth and fifth principles are not directly referred to in this account but are definitely present. They are *organization* and *faith*. The apostles increased their level of organization to meet the needs of the people. They not only trusted in the Spirit but also took concrete steps to order their world so as to increase its productivity. The apostles also had faith in God and the people. They trusted that the people would choose the right men, and that the Lord would help these men carry out this important job.

Something happened there that made the Church function properly. Those who ministered to the widows did so in the power of the Holy Spirit. Those who gave themselves to the Word and prayer did so with excellence. The number of disciples increased greatly, and the whole project was efficient. As they walked in faith, the apostles created an organization that was remarkable for its effectiveness, excellence, and efficiency.

Let's study these principles more closely so that each can become a part of your life, family, job, and ministry.

Chapter Two

"Waiting on Tables"

As we saw in the previous chapter, the apostles in Acts 6 had a few problems to solve. There was both good news and bad news in the Church, the piece of ground that God had given them to work. The good news was that the number of disciples was increasing. The word of the Lord was spreading rapidly and many were making decisions to follow Jesus. These conversions generated a lot of activity and ministry. The apostles, handpicked and trained by the Lord Himself, were the natural choices to train and direct the growth of these early disciples. Due to this explosive growth, they found themselves totally immersed in the life of this emerging body of believers.

Now for the bad news: Some of the widows were being overlooked in the daily distribution of food. The Grecian Jews, whose widows were not being taken care of, approached these leaders and apostles for help. That led to more bad news, for the apostles already had their hands full seeking God for direction on how to lead the new converts and continue to promote church growth. The Grecian Jews wanted action and perhaps expected these leaders to personally oversee the solution. What were the apostles to do?

Covey writes in *The 7 Habits of Highly Effective People:*

> It's incredibly easy to get caught up in an activity trap, in the busy-ness of life, to work harder and harder at climbing the ladder of success only to discover it's leaning against the wrong wall. It is possible to be busy—very busy—without being very effective.... How different our lives are when we really know what is deeply important to

4

us, and, keeping that picture in mind, we manage ourselves each day to be and to do what really matters most.
If the ladder is not leaning against the right wall, every
step we take just gets us to the wrong place faster. We may
be very busy, we may be very efficient, but we will also be
truly effective only when we begin with the end in mind.[1]

For Covey, the "end in mind" is determining what you want to
be known for and then preparing to actually do that very thing.
The apostles in Acts 6 had the "end in mind" and decided they
could not "wait on tables." Their purpose was *not* to minister to
the widows ("wait on tables") but, rather, to devote themselves to
the Word of God and prayer. They could have climbed the ladder
of this ministry of serving the widows only to find it leaning
against the wrong wall. The right spot for the apostles was the
place on the wall marked "the Word of God and prayer."

This section on effectiveness is subtitled, "Know Where To
Stake Your Claim." If the early gold miners were to find gold, it
was critical that they worked the proper piece of ground. Once
they found the right field, they had to stake a claim to show that
the field was theirs. Otherwise, they would lose all that they had
gained from their sacrifices. You, too, need to stake your claim
carefully and then work your claim. You will find true gold only
by giving yourself to the purpose God has set aside for you—that
is your field.

When verse four says that the apostles gave themselves to
"prayer and the ministry of the Word," it doesn't refer to the
normal devotional life that every believer is expected to maintain.
Certainly all the early believers were taught to pray and study the
Scriptures. The apostles, however, had a unique role to play in the
Word and prayer. They had been with Jesus, and things they saw
and were taught made them vital to the future of the covenant
community. They knew their purpose and said, "We can't get involved in this because we have to give ourselves to something
else." Waiting on tables would have taken them away from that
purpose.

Gold Nugget One

"Let your eyes look straight ahead, fix your gaze directly before you. Make level paths for your feet and take only ways that are firm. Do not swerve to the right or the left." —Proverbs 4:25-27

You need this same mentality, whether you're in the ministry or serving the Lord in some other area. You may be doing good things, even biblical things. But are you giving yourself to *the* thing that God has set aside for you to do? Have you staked your spiritual claim in the right field? If not, you need to say, like the apostles, "I can't do that. For me, that is waiting on tables." While writing this book, I've had to say "no" to other things, because this is what God has put before me. Anything else at this time would be "waiting on tables" for me.

You may have a good job that has given you a high standard of living, but perhaps you feel trapped and unfulfilled. If you're staying in that job because of the money, you're a hireling! If you're shuffling papers, when you really feel your purpose is to start a business, counsel, create artistic works, repair, or teach, then you are "waiting on tables" even if you're paid handsomely to do so.

Here's another example of what I mean. I have to be honest— as a pastor I didn't like hospital visitation. I used to jokingly tell the people I pastored, "If you want mercy, don't come to me. That's not my gift." I didn't mind going to see someone who was in my congregation. But when someone wanted me to visit the cousin of their aunt by marriage whom I had never met before, I started to think of all the things I could possibly be doing so that I could honestly say, "I'm busy."

I realize that as a disciple and brother I must develop mercy and compassion for others. But some of the expectations that people had for me as a pastor constituted "waiting on tables" for me. They had an idea of what a pastor should be and wanted me to fit their ideal.

You may think I'm unspiritual or wasn't really cut out to be a pastor because I didn't like hospital visitation. But I don't think that's the case at all. I would prefer to find a team of people who feel called to hospital ministry, from whom the gifts of mercy, faith, and intercession flow. Why not target those whose purpose it is to extend mercy and then let them do what they do best? They'll be fulfilling their purpose—and they'll also free me up so I can fulfill mine.

Peter Drucker, in his book, *The Effective Executive*, has a chapter entitled, "What Can I Contribute?" In so many words, he urges everyone in an organization to focus on what he or she is capable of contributing:

> The effective executive focuses on contribution.... The focus on contribution is the key to effectiveness: in a man's own work—its content, its level, its standards, and its impacts; in his relations with others—his superiors, his associates, his subordinates; in his use of the tools of the executive such as meetings or reports.... To focus on contribution is to focus on effectiveness.[2]

You can *best* contribute to any organization what you're gifted and divinely enabled to do, and that relates to your purpose.

Saying "no" to activities or projects can be difficult (and often not possible if your supervisor asks you to do something), but it's more difficult to continually function in something that's not your purpose. It's so easy, especially in the ministry, to get caught up in other people's expectations—the purpose *they* think you should have.

Can you picture the widows on the way to the meeting described in Acts 6? Perhaps they were talking on the way saying, "Peter is my favorite apostle. I love him so much. Peter will help me." Another widow was saying, "No, John is tops in my book. He's a dear, and I know that he'll do something." You can be sure that Peter and John responded, "We're sorry, but we can't help you because it will take us away from our purpose. However, we'll find someone else who can meet your needs."

A number of years ago, a movie called *Chariots of Fire* told the story of Eric Liddel, an Olympic runner, missionary to China, and eventual martyr. At one point in the film, Liddel's sister expressed her concern that he was devoting too much time to running. She was afraid it would take him away from his call as a missionary.

Liddel's response, while perhaps fictional, is still a classic. He told her that God made him fast. "And when I run," he said, "I feel His pleasure." What do you do that releases God's pleasure? Isn't that what you want to do as often as possible?

When I plan conferences, I feel God's pleasure. The Holy Spirit always helps me when I plan them; and time and again, God has covered my conference mistakes by His grace. I know His anointing will show up because conferences are part of my purpose (which I will describe in Chapter Four). When I "step to the plate" at a conference, I expect to hit a "home run." When I go to the hospital, on the other hand, I'm happy just to get to first base.

The heroes of the Bible knew their purpose and were able to concentrate on fulfilling it. That's why they were so successful. Let's turn now to a quick study of purpose in God's Word.

Chapter Three

God's Presence Reveals His Purpose

God is a God of purpose. I challenge you to find one person in the Bible to whom God appeared without revealing His purpose. God's presence and purpose go hand in hand. The presence of God isn't just a place to get goose bumps. Too many believers, I'm afraid, just want to go from spiritual high to high. When they can't find that high, they bounce from church to church. But my spiritual "high," if I may call it that, always comes from doing, at any given time, what I know I was born to do.

It's true that you will sometimes *feel* His presence, but that's not the end God has in mind. God's presence comes to *change* you and to help you better understand who He is and what He wants you to do.

Gold Nugget Two

"The Lord has made everything for its own purpose, even the wicked for the day of evil."—Proverbs 16:4 (NAS)

Let's examine some biblical examples. The Lord told **Adam** that his purpose was to "be fruitful and increase in number; fill the earth and subdue it" (Genesis 1:28); **Eve** was to be "a helper suitable" (Genesis 2:18) for Adam; **Abraham** was to be a great nation and a blessing to all the peoples of the earth (Genesis 12:2-3); **Joseph's** purpose was to rule over his father's sons (Genesis 37:8); **Moses** was "to bring my people the Israelites out of Egypt" (Exodus 3:10); the **nation of Israel** was to be the Lord's treasured possession, "a kingdom of priests and a holy nation" (Exodus 19:5-6); even **Pharaoh**, a heathen ruler, fulfilled God's purpose, for Exodus 9:16 says, "I have raised you [Pharaoh] up for this very purpose, that I might show you my power and that my name might be proclaimed in all the earth."

There are many more examples of God's presence and purpose acting as one. **Joshua** was to lead the people to inherit the promised land (Joshua 1:6); **David** was to be king of Israel (1 Samuel 16:12-13); **Isaiah** was to "go and tell this people" (Isaiah 6:9); **Jeremiah**, from before the womb, was appointed "as a prophet to the nations" (Jeremiah 1:5); and **Esther** was made queen to save her people from destruction, as her cousin Mordecai reminded her when he said, "Who knows but that you have come to royal position for such a time as this?" (Esther 4:14). It's of note that not all of these people were in "religious" work. Some were called by the Lord to function in secular positions (such as Esther).

We can also see God's calling and purpose in the New Testament. **John the Baptist** came to "prepare the way for the Lord, make straight paths for him" (Matthew 3:3). His purpose was so clear to him that, when the people declared him to be the Messiah, he insisted that he was not. Even when the offer of a "promotion" to Messiah came along, John knew what his purpose was and could not be diverted. **Peter** and **Andrew** were to be "fishers of men" (Matthew 4:19). Peter was also given "the keys of the kingdom of heaven" (Matthew 16:19).

Acts 13:36 says, "For when David *had served God's purpose* in his own generation, he fell asleep" (emphasis added). I can't find any place in the Old or New Testaments where God didn't reveal purpose when He revealed His presence to someone. It's my prayer that, like David, I too will serve God's purpose in my generation. When I go to sleep, I want to say like Paul, "I have finished the race, I have kept the faith" (2 Timothy 4:7). Like Paul, I want to know my course and know that I ran it well.

If God has called me to wait on tables (and it was the purpose for some in Acts 6), then I want to wait on tables so that the angels will marvel. But if tables are not my purpose, I want to avoid them like a plague.

How far can we take this concept? Let's take a look at John 17:1-5.

Father, the time has come. Glorify your Son, that your Son may glorify you. For you granted him authority over all people that he might give eternal life to all those you have given him. Now this is eternal life: that they may know you, the only true God, and Jesus Christ, whom you have sent. I have brought you glory on earth by completing the work you gave me to do. *And now, Father, glorify me in your presence with the glory I had with you before the world began* (emphasis added).

Jesus brought glory to the Father by doing the work He was sent to do. He didn't glorify God by singing and praising or by being doctrinally correct. He brought glory to God by being faithful to the purpose assigned Him by the Father. You'll glorify God in the same manner as you complete the work that has been set aside for you and you alone.

One day Jesus went to Jericho and found himself in the midst of a procession. A short man climbed up a tree to get a better look at what was going on. When Jesus passed by, He said, "Zacchaeus, come down immediately. I must stay at your house today" (Luke 19:5).

Zacchaeus obeyed and welcomed Him with a dinner. After dinner, Zacchaeus stood and announced, "Look, Lord! Here and now I give half of my possessions to the poor, and if I have cheated anybody out of anything, I will pay back four times the amount" (Luke 19:8).

Imagine the shock among the people, especially his fellow tax collectors. But Jesus responded, "Today salvation has come to this house, because this man, too, is a son of Abraham. *For the Son of Man came to seek and to save what was lost*" (Luke 19:9-10, emphasis added).

Jesus' purpose was summarized in that simple statement. The people tried to make Him a king, a political deliverer, and a rabbi. Yet He resisted all those titles and roles because they weren't consistent with His purpose. When He ran to the lost, so to speak, He felt God's pleasure. But He told the Pharisees, "I have not come to call the righteous, but sinners" (Matthew 9:13).

It can be argued that Jesus came to fully realize His purpose the same way you will realize yours—by seeking God. As a 12-year-old, Jesus was in the temple seeking His purpose. He had to be about His Father's business, but first He had to know what that business was. Was it to ride into Jerusalem on a white stallion? To restore Israel politically? To show forth the Father's power by great miracles and public displays?

Jesus found His purpose and focused on it the same way you will find yours. He set His face like flint to find it and then do it. Hebrews 12:2 says, "For the joy set before him, He endured the cross, scorning its shame, and sat down at the right hand of the throne of God." For the joy of the purpose that was assigned to Him, He went through all kinds of grief. Today He still seeks and saves the lost, and you and I are certainly glad for that.

Gold Nugget Three

"If you call out for insight and cry aloud for understanding, and if you look for it as for silver and search for it as for hidden treasure, then you will understand the fear of the Lord and find the knowledge of God." —Proverbs 2:3-5

Covey maintains that "we have the initiative and the responsibility to make things happen."[3] This isn't altogether true and misses the concept that, for the believer, all things initiate in the will of God. If the believer is to "make things happen," it isn't because he or she decided to do so. It's because the Lord put that desire to "make things happen" in them in the first place. Jesus didn't come out of His own will; He came in response to the Father's will and submitted His will to that.

Covey also states,

> Frankl says we *detect* rather than *invent* our missions in life. I like that choice of words. I think each of us has an internal monitor or sense, a *conscience*, that gives us an awareness of our own uniqueness and the singular contributions that we can make. In Frankl's words, "Everyone has his own specific vocation or mission in life.... Therein he cannot be replaced, nor can his life be repeated. Thus, everyone's task is as unique as is his specific opportunity to implement it."[4]

Unfortunately, Covey uses the word *conscience* in a totally un-biblical manner. And neither Covey nor Frankl can say how this vocation or mission is programmed into an individual's life. The Christian believer, however, knows that God the Father assigns this unique mission.

Jesus wasn't looking to develop His potential or to assert His will to be all that He could be. He said on one occasion, "My food is to do the will of Him who sent me and to finish His work" (John 4:34); and on another, "I did not speak of my own accord, but the Father who sent me commanded me *what to say and how to say it* (John 12:49, emphasis added). When Covey writes, "We are responsible for our own effectiveness, for our own happiness, and ultimately, I would say, for most of our circumstances,"[5] his philosophy is contrary to what we see in Jesus' life.

The apostles were undoubtedly impacted by Jesus' sense of purpose. In Acts 6 they had determined what *their* purpose was, and they could not be diverted from this purpose to wait on tables. As time went on, each apostle saw more clearly that they were to devote themselves to prayer and the Word. This basic purpose never changed, even though they carried it out in different places and in different ways. But through it all, they turned the world upside down.

The apostles didn't just decide to "make things happen." They cooperated with the will of God that existed for their life before the world began. And the Holy Spirit led them and worked in them to bring about such fantastic results.

Not only did the apostles know their purpose, but they could also plainly state it. Look at Galatians 2:7-9:

> *They saw that I had been entrusted with the task of preaching the gospel to the Gentiles, just as Peter had been to the Jews. For God, who was at work in the ministry of Peter as an apostle to the Jews, was also at work in my ministry as an apostle to the Gentiles.*

Paul knew his purpose, and he also knew Peter's purpose. Each one's mission was so well defined that others knew what it was and respected it. In fact, Paul's purpose was so clear to him that he refused to baptize people. In 1 Corinthians 1:14 and 17, he states, "I am thankful that I did not baptize any of you...For Christ did not send me to baptize but to preach the gospel." (Now I don't feel so guilty about not wanting to do hospital visitation!)

Furthermore, in Romans 15:20 and 22 Paul wrote,

> *It has always been my ambition to preach the gospel where Christ was not known, so that I would not be building on someone else's foundation . . .This is why I have often been hindered from coming to you.*

Paul's mission was to preach to the Gentiles who had never heard of Christ. When he tried to go to Rome, a trip that at the time was not consistent with his purpose, God resisted him!

Paul loved that church, but for him Rome was the equivalent of "waiting on tables." The only way he thought he would get there was stated in Romans 15:24: "I plan to do so [visit the Roman church] when I go to Spain. I hope to visit you while passing through." Paul thought he could get to Rome as he went to the un-evangelized people of Spain. Instead, he got there after he appealed to Caesar, since evangelizing kings and leaders was part of his purpose.

You have a purpose, just like Adam, Abraham, David, Daniel and Paul. Ephesians 4:16 says, "From whom the whole body, joined and knit together by what every joint supplies, according to the effective working by which *every part does its share*, causes growth of the body for the edifying of itself in love" (NKJV, emphasis added).

The word "effective" in that verse means that each part supplies what only it can supply. When that happens, the Body is effective. And remember, Adam, Esther, and Daniel didn't function as religious leaders and you may not either. But you will strengthen the Body by being who God made you to be, even though your main thrust may be in another area of life.

John Wooden, former college basketball coach at UCLA, once said, "Do not let what you cannot do interfere with what you can do." Don't feel as if you need to be everything to everyone. You don't have to do all the ministry. And you don't need to be president of the company to be successful. You just have to be faithful to your purpose and please God by so doing.

Think of this analogy from the sports world. No football team wants a quarterback who can do it all. The quarterback doesn't need to also be the defensive back, tight end, and halfback. What the team wants and needs is a quarterback who can throw the ball and lead the team downfield. It's the same with the body of Christ. The body of Christ doesn't need well-rounded people. The Body needs people who are specialists, who know their purpose and have given themselves to it wholeheartedly.

First Corinthians 3:13 says, "His work shall be shown for what it is, because the Day will bring it to light. It will be revealed with fire, and the fire will test the quality of each man's work." The fire will test your work. I have often wondered if burnout is a result of the fire of God that tests your work every now and then. This fire may reveal something that you are involved in that you don't need to be involved in. If you can identify what you still have energy to do while suffering from burnout, you're well on your way to knowing what your life purpose is. The work you did out of guilt, anxiety, pride, or ignorance burns up like wood, hay, and stubble.

With this in mind, let's look at some simple steps that you can take to identify or clarify your purpose.

Chapter Four

Finding the Road That Leads to Your Purpose

There's an old saying that "the longest journey begins with one step." There are practical steps you can take that will help you identify and define your God-given purpose. They are the same steps that Nehemiah took to find and confirm what God called him to do. You may want to read the book of Nehemiah before you read this chapter. As you read, ask yourself, "How can I find this sense of destiny? How can I sort out my world and life as Nehemiah did, get to the place of purpose that he got to, and state my mission with certainty?"

After you have read Nehemiah, consider the following four points.

1. **Nehemiah sought the Lord for his purpose.** You may not be aware of your purpose because you've never asked the Lord to clarify it for you. Nehemiah 1:4 says, "When I heard these things, I sat down and wept. For some days I mourned and fasted and prayed before the God of heaven." It was in that posture that Nehemiah saw what God wanted him to do.

Gold Nugget Four

"It is the glory of God to conceal a matter;
to search out a matter is the glory of kings." —Proverbs 25:2

Perhaps Nehemiah was familiar with Proverbs 2:3-5, a Gold Nugget mentioned earlier: "If you *call out* for insight and *cry aloud* for understanding, and *if you look for it* as for silver and *search for it* as for hidden treasure, then you will understand the fear of the Lord and find the knowledge of God" (emphasis added). That's what seeking the Lord is like.

You must cry aloud and earnestly seek the Lord with all your being. For instance, the congregation I pastored set aside January for prayer and fasting. We usually fasted for 21 days and had regular prayer times. I was always amazed how God allowed Himself to be found during those times; He was faithful to reveal Himself in response to our diligent search.

The New Testament confirms what Proverbs 2 teaches. Hebrews 11:6 says, "Without faith it is impossible to please God, because anyone who comes to him must believe that he exists and that he rewards those who earnestly [diligently] seek him." If you seek the Lord with all you have, you will find Him. Or perhaps it's better to say that He will allow Himself to be found.

You may already know your purpose, or be closer to knowing it than you realize. Often it's the thing that you see clearly and do with ease. You can easily take your purpose for granted because to you it's second nature. What do you do that causes people to say, "Wow, how did you do that?"? You probably reply, "It was nothing." In a sense, it was nothing to you because it was consistent with your purpose. For you it comes naturally, and for that reason you may consider it insignificant.

Nehemiah's purpose, for example, was to rebuild Jerusalem, the city of his fathers, which is why he asked visitors how it was "back home." Everyone else was carrying on with business as usual, but Nehemiah had a burden for Jerusalem. The visitors' report that the city was in ruins devastated Nehemiah more than anyone else. That report simply helped make it clear to him what he was to do about that situation back home.

You don't have to make national headlines, preach like Billy Graham, minister like Mother Teresa, or sing like Amy Grant to be successful in the eyes of God. Consider Dorcas, whose death and resurrection are described in Acts 9:36-43. Dorcas was a woman of means and a seamstress who "was always doing good and helping the poor." That was her purpose; she gave herself to it and did an effective job.

When Dorcas died, her friends summoned Peter, the apostle to the Jews and arguably the best-known apostle of the day. He was a great man of God who went to pay his respects to a small-town seamstress. When he arrived at her house, he found everybody weeping. The widows showed him the clothes Dorcas had made for them, proof that she had faithfully carried out her mission. Peter was so moved by a woman given to her purpose that he went in, prayed, and told her to "get up." Dorcas, who ministered to an insignificant group of people in a nowhere town, received all the resources of heaven in her hour of need because she had been faithful to her God-given purpose.

I wonder if Dorcas ever thought, "The only thing I know how to do is sew. That cloak was nothing. Please accept it as my gift." Perhaps she thought that what she did was nothing special, but, in reality, her handiwork was the result of divine empowerment. She did what she did best and blessed many people through her purpose. You have the same potential.

How about a man named Joseph who is mentioned in the Book of Acts? You probably don't know him as Joseph, because his name was changed by the apostles. This Joseph gave himself so wholeheartedly to his purpose that people took it upon themselves to change his name!

We read in Acts 4:36-37:

Joseph, a Levite from Cyprus, whom the apostles called Barnabas (which means Son of Encouragement), sold a field he owned and brought the money and put it at the apostles' feet.

Put yourself in the apostles' place in those early days. Maybe they had a rough day, and the secretary informed them that they had one appointment remaining. When they heard it was Joseph, they said, "Oh, you mean Barnabas, the Son of Encouragement. Every time we see him he encourages us. Show him in."

At that point, Joseph came in holding two bags of money and placed them at the apostles' feet. He said, "I had this piece of land and I thought I would sell it and give the money to you to do with as you wish. I appreciate the job you're doing and I love you all."

When he left, the apostles were glad they had let him in. He refreshed and encouraged them and was true to the new name he had been given. From that point on, every time we read of Barnabas, he is living up to his name.

When the early church wouldn't have anything to do with Saul, Barnabas came forward and encouraged them to accept him (Acts 9:27). When the work in Antioch among the Gentiles was exploding, the apostles sent Barnabas there.

When he arrived and saw the evidence of the grace of God, he was glad and encouraged *them all to remain true to the Lord with all their hearts. He was a good man, full of the Holy Spirit and faith, and a great number of people were brought to the Lord* (Acts 11:23-24 emphasis added).

Barnabas wasn't interested in keeping that work in Antioch all to himself, so he "went to Tarsus to look for Saul, and when he found him, he brought him to Antioch" (Acts 11:25-26). Barnabas took that opportunity to encourage Saul and his ministry.

Barnabas had more than a gift of encouragement. Even though he was a teacher, apostle, prophet, evangelist, and giver, he encouraged people in the midst of it all. When he ran to encourage people, he felt God's pleasure.

Bolles in *What Color is Your Parachute?* writes,

We need to unlearn the idea that our unique Mission must consist of some achievement which all the world will see, and learn instead that as the stone does not always know what ripples it has caused in the pond whose surface it impacts, so neither we nor those who watch our life will always know *what we have achieved* by our life and by our Mission. *It may be* that by the grace of God we helped bring about a profound change for the better in the lives of other souls around us, but it also may be that this takes place beyond our sight, or after we have gone on. And we may never know what we have accomplished, until we see Him face-to-face after this life is past.[6]

I doubt if Dorcas expected to be memorialized in the written Word of God for all generations because of what she did. But she was, and we are the richer for her story.

Nehemiah operated in the same power that comes when anyone functions in purpose. He sought the Lord for his purpose; in fact, he agonized over it. You can't read his opening prayer in

Nehemiah 1:5-11 without feeling his agony as he poured out his heart before the Lord. He was diligent to seek and the Lord revealed his purpose.

2. **Nehemiah saw himself as part of a larger group**. Nehemiah didn't pray *I* prayers; he prayed *we* prayers. He said things like, "I confess the sins *we* have committed against you," "*We* have acted wickedly," and "*We* have not obeyed your commands." His fathers and grandfathers had abandoned the covenant, and as a result Nehemiah was serving in a foreign land, far away from Judah, through no apparent fault of his own. But he was still praying "we" because he saw himself as part of a larger body.

Gold Nugget Five

"He who separates himself seeks his own desire,
he quarrels against all sound wisdom." —Proverbs 18:1

You need to see yourself in the same way. If you find yourself fulfilling your mission in the secular world, be a team player. Don't stand off and judge those with whom you work. Be a part of their lives and have the best interests of the organization at heart. Nehemiah served a heathen king and appears to have done it with distinction. Daniel gave his best to Nebuchadnezzar, the man who had ransacked his nation and radically changed his life. God expects you to give your best to your "world" as well, even if it is part of the world's system.

I learned this when I was secularly employed prior to entering the ministry. I found myself working at a chain of trade schools as the admissions director, and some of the students and co-workers had some serious problems. With those problems came the smoking, cursing, and perverted lifestyles that are all too common in the world.

I had a serious problem with one of my supervisors whose lifestyle was one that I found particularly troublesome and offensive. This man would order me to do things, yelling out my name from down the hall in a mocking tone. I tried to stay away from him as much as possible, but our paths still crossed more often than I liked.

While on this job, I was paid a commission, only to have my

commissions dry up about one year after I took the job. I began praying for my financial needs and the Holy Spirit revealed to me that my bad attitude toward that supervisor had caused my financial lack.

I tried to reason with the Lord, but He would not relent. My finances did not improve until I repented of my attitude toward that man. When I did, not only did my finances improve, but my ability to work with my supervisor and other people improved. I saw how judgmental I had been, and I realized some of what Jesus must have encountered when He came to us. The sinless Son of God had to deal daily with imperfect men and women, yet He did so with grace and mercy. I was called to follow in His footsteps, and that job and supervisor gave me the perfect chance to do just that.

If you have found your purpose being fulfilled in church work, you too need to have the correct attitude. The Church is the apple of God's eye. Jesus didn't give Himself for you to stay in individualism. He gave Himself to build the Church. It's the Church that the gates of hell will try to prevail against unsuccessfully.

There are many hurt people today who were wounded in church splits and mistakes. Without question, there have been serious problems with leaders, elders, pastors, deacons, and staff members.

If you've been hurt, you need to follow Nehemiah's example. You need to work through your hurt and anger to a place of healing and release. Then you need to get on with your purpose, which may take place for you in and through the Church. There's an entire generation today that doesn't really care what you've been through. When you compare what you've been through to the hell where they're going, you can see the importance of finding and functioning in your purpose. You also understand why the devil has so attacked the Church to render her weak and without purpose.

You may be thinking, "You don't know...I did so much...and the pastor brought his brother-in-law in and fired me. It was so unfair and painful." That's the way it can be when you are involved with imperfect people. It may not have been fair, but that's life in the real world. The Church has been an imperfect place filled with imperfect people for 2000 years, and it's not going to change any time soon. The Bible is full of instructions on how to handle your hurt. Withdrawal and isolation are not among your options.

I can relate to some of your pain and disillusionment in this area as well. Several years ago, I was "let go" from a Christian ministry. I had given a few years of my life to it, and now I was out. I reacted in anger, moved my office equipment home by myself, and found myself sitting in my office at home every morning pouting and depressed.

One morning the Holy Spirit spoke to me as clearly as He ever had and said, "You're not dealing with that ministry; you're dealing with Me. I sent you home." That statement saved my life and delivered me from destructive bitterness and anger. All of a sudden I saw that God had released me from that job because I wasn't needed there anymore. He had something else for me to do—a new way to apply my purpose—and He used that incident to get me in position for my next step. If I had been listening more closely to Him, I probably would have resigned before I was let go. I wasn't listening, however, and God had to use extraordinary means to get my attention.

Shortly after that release I got an invitation to pastor a church in Orlando, Florida, where I served for four wonderful years. I began writing this book in Orlando, pastoring in a city I loved, surrounded by people I loved, and doing things I always dreamed of doing!

I was dealing with God—and you have been, too. God loves His Church and wants you to love it, too, regardless of what has happened. Whether you were hurt attending or working for a church, you need to have the same attitude as Joseph toward those who have hurt you. He told his brothers, "You intended to harm me, but God intended it for good to accomplish what is now being done, the saving of many lives" (Genesis 50:20).

Compare that with what Nehemiah could have said: "*My fathers* sinned and *they* did these things wrong." No! Instead he prayed, "We, we, we!" Because he had a right heart attitude, God clearly revealed to him that he was to have a role in the rebuilding process. Only "we" people get that privilege.

3. **Nehemiah confessed his inability to accomplish his purpose**. When I hear someone talking about purpose, I like to sense

some humility. You must realize that God doesn't want you to trust in your own abilities, but in Him. If there is no awe for the purpose, there at least needs to be a healthy respect for the obstacles that must be overcome to accomplish it. God will not place you in your comfort zone. Your purpose will require faith and diligence if you are to be effective.

Nehemiah went to Jerusalem and surveyed how much needed to be done. His enemies rose up to discourage him, but he told them, "The God of heaven will give us success" (2:20). He had to pray constantly and ask God's help. The people had to work with a sword in one hand in case of attack. When they finished the wall in 52 days, Nehemiah wrote that "all the surrounding nations were afraid and lost their self-confidence, *because they realized that this work had been done with the help of our God*" (6:16, emphasis added). He knew that his effectiveness was found in God helping him do what he was created to do.

Abraham was certainly overwhelmed by his purpose to be a father of a multitude. Moses came to the place where he could not lead the people without God's help. Solomon prayed for wisdom to lead Israel. Jeremiah tried to escape doing what he was to do, and God had to deal with him severely.

Everyone in the Bible was overwhelmed by their purpose. Even Jesus sweat drops of blood when He came to the hour in which His purpose would be fulfilled. Angels came and ministered to Him in the garden to strengthen Him for the cross. But the burden was almost too much.

In light of this company, do you think that your purpose will be a trip down easy street? In all probability it will take you out of yourself and press you into the Lord like never before.

4. **Nehemiah was able to clearly describe his purpose to the king**. If you aren't clear about your purpose, other people won't be clear about it either. You need to have a statement that explains your purpose in one clear, concise sentence. Until you have that, you can't be fully effective because your focus will not be sharp. You will still have the tendency to be distracted or spread too thin.

Nehemiah, the king's butler, came before the king with a sad face. The king asked, "Why does your face look so sad when you are not ill?" (2:2). Nehemiah responded that he was upset over the state of affairs in Jerusalem. The king then asked the crucial question, *"What is it you want?"* (2:4, emphasis added).

Praise God that Nehemiah didn't back down, or play religious games and say something like, "I just want the Lord to use me." Instead, he asked to be sent to the city of his fathers! He further requested supplies and letters of passage. The king finally asked, "How long will your journey take?" and Nehemiah "set a time" (2:6). He was specific. He knew what he was to do, what he needed to accomplish, and how much time it would take to finish it. He was specific in prayer and with men because he knew his purpose.

Clarifying my own purpose came as I went through a painful failure a number of years ago. At that time I was part of a team that started a "Christian" business. Our goals for our profits were simple and direct: We were going to make money for the kingdom of God, fund missions projects, and provide jobs only for the brothers and sisters in the church. With those goals, we just knew we couldn't fail, for God would certainly be with us.

We started the business and things went sour more quickly than we could ever have imagined. We spent $25,000 with very few sales to show for it. Soon all those involved went to look for other work. The business folded shortly thereafter, and because my name was on the office and phone system leases, guess who got stuck with the bills?

One morning I was praying, "Oh God, save this business for Your glory!" I felt the Holy Spirit respond gently as the thought shot through my mind, "You're not interested in My glory. You're interested in saving your own neck."

That was absolutely true, and I angrily responded to the Lord, "If You didn't call me to start this business, then what did You call me to do?"

Immediately, I felt impressed to turn to Genesis 1:2, which says, "Now the earth was formless and empty, darkness was over the surface of the deep, and the Spirit of God was hovering over the waters." When I studied that verse in a commentary, it stated that the Spirit brought order out of the chaos found in the earth's condition. Suddenly, I was confronted with my own purpose: *To bring order out of chaos.*

I almost fell to the ground. It was so clear, concise, and direct. When I was a child, I would empty my dad's garage, sweep it out, put everything back in order, and then feel an awesome sense of peace when I stood back and looked at everything in place. That tendency continued as an adult as I realized that every job I ever had was a job no one else had done. I was always given new positions so that I could *bring order out of chaos.* Even before I was a believer, I was fulfilling my purpose and didn't know it! *Bringing order out of chaos* was my life purpose!

In most cases, your purpose is accompanied by a verse or passage of Scripture that gives a biblical summary for what you were born to do. When Jesus was in the synagogue in Nazareth where he was raised…

> …*the scroll of the prophet Isaiah was handed to him. Unrolling it, he found the place where it is written: "The Spirit of the Lord is on me, because he has anointed me to preach good news to the poor. He has sent me to proclaim freedom for the prisoners and recovery of sight for the blind, to release the oppressed, to proclaim the year of the Lord's favor"* (Luke 4:17-19).

After he sat down, he said, "Today this scripture is fulfilled in your hearing" (verse 21). Jesus had a passage that summarized what His purpose was.

When an invitation first came for me to be involved in prison ministry, I felt released to do so because there was a lot of chaos in the inmates' lives; that ministry was consistent with my purpose. A ministry I assisted in South America was in need of structure and purpose when I first got involved. My call to Orlando was to come and pastor the church because it needed definition and purpose. All these ministry opportunities fit into my purpose of helping structure lives and institutions that have little or no structure. None of them came because I chose them. When I work to bring order out of chaos, I'm effective and have power to achieve results. You might say that when I work with chaos, I feel God's pleasure.

I know that you desire that same clarity, but getting there isn't always an easy process. Let's turn our attention now to some of the major obstacles you face as you seek your mission or purpose statement.

Chapter Five

Roadblocks on the Road to Purpose

Finding your purpose is not always easy. Finding my own purpose came out of a painful business failure. In fact, the process can be so difficult that many don't even bother to search for it. Others don't want to be responsible for what they find. Still others don't want to be restricted because they enjoy "freelancing"— doing a little of this and a little of that. Let's look at some of the roadblocks you may encounter as you seek to find and clarify your purpose.

1. **Don't confuse "tent making" with your purpose**. I asked a young lady one time what her purpose was and she responded without thought, "I'm a secretary." Don't assume that your job is your purpose. You're undoubtedly performing a job that pays your bills, but that doesn't mean you should take your identity from it. William Carey, the great missionary pioneer, once said, "My business is to witness for Christ. I make shoes to pay my expenses."

If people had asked Paul what his purpose was, I doubt that he would have responded, "I'm a tent maker." He did make tents, but his purpose was to preach to the Gentiles. He used tent making to accomplish his purpose. Nehemiah wasn't a butler; he was the rebuilder of Jerusalem. Once you see your purpose, it will help you endure a job that may even be a source of frustration for you. Having a proper understanding of your purpose will also keep you from feeling as if you're not serving the Lord just because you're employed in a secular position.

My wife's sister is a writer. When she was working for a Christian magazine years ago, she took a standardized spiritual gifts test because she was trying to clarify her purpose. Her test results showed that she was strong in missions and hospitality (which was a confirmation of what she had always enjoyed doing), and that stimulated her thinking. She began to ask herself how she could fulfill her purpose as a missionary while employed in Mobile, Alabama. The Lord soon showed her how to serve college students from foreign countries, and she began to specifically target students from mainland China.

Today she continues to fulfill her purpose to the Chinese in Florida where she is a freelance writer. She has edited a newspaper directed to Chinese students and also writes articles and books that serve to heighten the awareness of people to the needs and opportunities of Chinese missions. She doesn't see herself primarily as a writer, although that's how she makes her living. She's a missionary and has found creative, Spirit-led ways to do what she was born to do.

Married women are particularly vulnerable to this identity crisis because they tend to draw their purpose from their day-to-day activities and routine. Housekeeping and raising children can fall under the category of "tent making." That's what consumes most of a homemaker's time, but are those activities her divine purpose? A woman's children or husband can be called home to heaven at any time. If that happens, is her purpose over?

Anna found herself in this very situation in Luke 2:36-38. She was married for seven years when her husband died. But her purpose didn't die with him. Instead, she served in the temple and "worshiped night and day, fasting and praying." Anna was 84 years old when Mary and Joseph came to the temple. She ministered effectively and waited to see the hope of Israel. Women have purpose *before* they meet their spouses and *after* they have children.

My wife enjoys the world of business. When our children were young, however, she stayed home with them. She was then and still is a wonderful mother and homemaker, and I greatly admire her. She was also a great pastor's wife. Yet she has a purpose that is beyond our home.

It's obvious that her purpose is not to counsel, teach, or serve in the church nursery on Sunday because when she has had to prepare a lesson to teach, we all suffer as she struggles with it. But my wife's purpose does lie in the business world.

Her purpose came home clearly at a time when our children

were small. She had a business idea and began to venture into the woods, drag home grapevines, and fashion them into round and heart-shaped wreaths of all sizes. One thing led to another and, before we knew what happened, she had grossed almost $8,000 in annual sales while working out of her kitchen making wreaths. God anointed her as she functioned in her purpose. We know that her destiny lies in the business world, and we pray for God to open the door for her there.

2. **Don't underestimate your ability to work**. The 40-hour work week is a modern phenomenon, a product of technology and union negotiations. If you work in the energy and power of God, you can do more than you ever thought possible! You can work 16-hour days and still be effective. On at least one occasion, Paul preached all night because his purpose compelled him to move on the next day. During that sermon, a young man sank into a deep sleep and fell to the ground from the third story because Paul preached so long (see Acts 20). But Paul raised him up and kept right on functioning in his purpose of preaching to the Gentiles. Paul wrote that he endured "in hard work, sleepless nights and hunger" (2 Corinthians 6:5).

Years ago I was pastoring a church of 50 people. That kept me busy enough, but I also found myself serving as church administrator. In addition, I had family responsibilities, and was involved in several community service projects. In the midst of all that, I was asked to consider being the administrator for another ministry without relinquishing any of the responsibilities I already had.

There was no way I could do it all, or so I thought. I began to seek the Lord about my many duties and what I should eliminate. One morning I awoke with 1 Corinthians 15:10 on my mind. I didn't know what that verse said, and I hadn't been reading Corinthians lately. I went right to the Bible and found the answer to the questions I'd been asking God: "By the grace of God, I am what I am, and His grace to me was not without effect. No, I worked harder than all of them—yet not I, but the grace of God that was with me."

The Lord was clearly telling me that there wasn't going to be any *less* to do. In fact, He increased my duties without taking any away. He wanted to teach me how to handle an enlarged sphere!

If God wants you to go back to school, for instance, don't say, "I can't because classes are at night, and I'll be away from my family. It will cut into this or that." Go to school. You may be concerned that you won't have time to study, but you won't know that for sure until you get into it. At one point in my life, I was pastoring a church, traveling as event coordinator for Worship International, serving as executive director for the Julio Ruibal Foundation (a missions group stationed in Colombia, South America), and functioning as president of the board of Rivers of Living Water Prison Ministries.

At the same time, I was also working on my doctorate in pastoral ministry from Liberty Theological Seminary in Houston, Texas. I was the assistant scoutmaster for my son's Boy Scout troop, and I was able to attend many of my daughter's school activities (and she was involved in quite a few).

It was difficult sometimes to juggle all those activities, but they all came out of my purpose; I felt God had directed me to each of them. But in order to do them all well, I had to let other things go. There wasn't much time for television, for example, and I couldn't watch sports as I had previously.

It was hard, but it can be done. If I did it, so can you, because the same grace is available to you. Take a look at 1 Corinthians 3:13: "His work will be shown for what it is." The word "work" is the Greek word *kopos*. It literally means "a beating of the breast with grief." It is also translated as "intense labor united with toil and trouble." That is what comes with purpose—hard work with some measure of trouble.

A few years ago, an issue of *Christian History* magazine was devoted to "The Golden Age of Hymns" and featured articles about the great hymn writers of the past. One paragraph in that issue captured my attention. It told of William Cowper, who composed 68 hymns in his lifetime; John Newton, who wrote 280; Philip Doddridge, who produced almost 400; and Isaac Watts, who wrote 697. Charles Wesley, however, wrote 8,989 hymns![7]

Wesley didn't have a computer, FAX machine, or telephone. He wrote some hymns on horseback while going from one revival to the next. Charles Wesley was a man who knew his purpose. He was effective, worked long and hard, and has impacted many people for more than 200 years!

John Wesley, Charles' brother, was known as the founder of the Methodist movement. Again, *Christian History* magazine gives us insight into the secret of John Wesley's effectiveness by providing this quote from his journal:

This being my birth-day, the first day of my seventy second year, I was considering, How is this, that I find just the same strength as I did thirty years ago? That my sight is considerably better now, and my nerves firmer than they were then? That I have none of the infirmities of old age, and have lost several I had in my youth? The grand cause is, the good pleasure of God, who doth whatsoever pleaseth him. The chief means are, 1, my constantly rising at four, for about fifty years: 2, my generally preaching at five in the morning, one of the most healthy exercises in the world: 3, my never travelling less, by sea or land, than four thousand five hundred miles a year.[8]

We are then told that "during his ministry, John Wesley road over 250,000 miles on horseback, a distance equal to ten circuits of the globe along the equator. He preached over 40,000 sermons."[9]

Don't underestimate your capacity to work. Allow the Holy Spirit to be released as you carry out your purpose. There are songs to be written, degrees to be earned, musical instruments to be learned, and new languages to be mastered. If you can see these as part of your purpose and find a way to release the grace and power of God, you can do it! You will be effective!

3. **Don't pursue or pray for the purpose that you *want* or *hope* to have**. That is a serious hindrance to finding your true purpose. Churches get torn apart at times because the associate wants to be pastor and the youth director wants more responsibility. I've seen men and women quit their jobs because they felt the jobs weren't spiritual enough. You can sincerely feel that you know your purpose and yet be sincerely wrong. Sincerity is not the judge of accuracy.

This actually happened to the Apostle Paul. Look at Acts 22:12-21:

A man named Ananias came to see me. He was a devout ob-
server of the law and highly respected by all the Jews living
there. He stood beside me and said, "Brother Saul, receive your
sight!" And at that very moment I was able to see him. Then he
said, "The God of our fathers has chosen you to know his will
and to see the Righteous One and to hear words from his mouth.
You will be his witness to all men of what you have seen and
heard. And now what are you waiting for? Get up, be baptized
and wash your sins away, calling on his name." When I re-
turned to Jerusalem and was praying at the temple, I fell into a
trance and saw the Lord speaking. "Quick!" he said to me.
"Leave Jerusalem immediately, because they will not accept your
testimony about me." "Lord," I replied, "these men know that I
went from one synagogue to another to imprison and beat those
who believe in you. And when the blood of your martyr Stephen
was shed, I stood there giving my approval and guarding the
clothes of those who were killing him." Then the Lord said to me,
"Go; I will send you far away to the Gentiles."

What was Paul doing in Jerusalem? I believe he was pursuing
the purpose he *wanted* or *hoped* to have. To paraphrase Paul, he
was saying, "God's going to send me to my people, the Jews. I am
a Jew's Jew. I'm already here in the temple. They all know I perse-
cuted the disciples. They'll know something happened on the
road. You see, Lord, this is what I want to do for You. This is
where You can best use me and it makes the most sense to me.
And by the way, this is also where I feel most comfortable."

God responded to Paul by ordering him to leave Jerusalem. It
would have cost Paul his life to stay there, and it will cost you
something to be involved in a purpose or pursuit not ordained by
God. You will be busy but not effective. As stated earlier, Proverbs
28:19 states, "He who works his land will have abundant food, but
the one who chases fantasies will have his fill of poverty." You
have a plot of land to work. It belongs to you and you alone. If you
work it, God will give you all that you need to get the job done.
Any other field is a fantasy for you and will trap you in unfruitful
busy-ness.

When I pray about things related to my purpose, I get results.
The Lord has given me cars, cellular phones, computers, books,

travel opportunities, spiritual insight, and much more because I needed them to work my "land." When I have chased "fantasies" (such as the wrong business opportunity), I've only gotten frustrated.

When I entered the ministry, I was one of the youngest members of a 20-man full-time staff. I remember thinking that 19 men stood in front of me before I would ever get a chance to minister. In 11 years, I seldom got to preach; but truthfully, I would not have had much to say. That "field" wasn't mine.

One day I was reading the local newspaper and saw an announcement for a meeting of the Public Relations Council of Alabama (PRCA). The words jumped out at me, and I sensed the Holy Spirit say, "Go to that meeting. That's your field."

Believe me, I didn't want to go to that meeting because I knew there would be a lot of unbelievers there. I knew I would probably be uncomfortable around them, and I knew they surely would be uncomfortable around me. In my mind, I had a complete scenario of what would happen the moment I stepped inside the door; yet I knew God was telling me to go, so I went.

The first person who saw me and realized that I was a visitor walked over and introduced herself. When I told her my name and that I was with a local church, she immediately tried to hide her cigarette and put down her drink. I don't know who was more uncomfortable—she or I! That afternoon I told the Lord that this wasn't going to work! But the Lord would not relent. It was three or four months before He "persuaded" me to go back again.

I started going to this meeting on a regular basis and gave myself to working that "field." Eventually I became president of the local chapter and then a member of the state board of directors. Over the years, I had the opportunity to counsel and pray with many of the members, and when I entered our church's magazine in a state competition sponsored by this organization, it won first place!

When I left that church to take another pastorate out of state, I sent the local PRCA members invitations to my farewell service. Some of them came and heard me preach. Whenever I did anything for that organization, the power of God was evident. There was no power for me to minister in my church—that was not my field. PRCA was my field, and it bore a lot of fruit. With the Lord's help, I was able to function in my purpose of bringing some order out of chaos in that situation.

As mentioned earlier, God is working today as He did in Daniel's time. He wants to send you to the Nebuchadnezzars of your day. Nebuchadnezzar was probably a hot-tempered, foul-mouthed idolater. It's amazing that *God* was the one who sent Daniel to work with that king. Daniel's purpose wasn't fulfilled in carrying out the requirements of the law in Jerusalem. Daniel was a righteous man, but his purpose was fulfilled in Babylon. He became the chief of the Babylonian wise men.

Can you imagine what Daniel's business meetings were like? Can you see him at the head of the table conducting the meeting? Perhaps the meeting went something like this: "All right, we will have our report now from the necromancers. And next let's hear from the astrologers. What's going on in your sphere? What's going on over here with the soothsayers, and what are the wise men of Babylon saying?" Daniel had to put up with wickedness, foolishness, sin, and evil men. But that's where God put him. He excelled in the midst of it all and was exalted.

I developed the *Life Is a Gold Mine* seminar in 1985 and presented it in congregations around the country. It was well received and seemed anointed, but suddenly the invitations stopped coming. I didn't teach the seminar again for several years. When I started teaching it again, it was for prison inmates! Perhaps the invitations had stopped coming because I was teaching in those early years out of ego and pride. I was a great teacher who was finally getting his chance—or so I thought.

The seminar was restored to me when I realized that the Lord gave it to me to help me accomplish my purpose. *Life Is a Gold Mine* was given to me to bring order out of chaos, not to inflate my already healthy ego. When I got that straight, I was able to get back to the business of teaching others about purpose.

4. **Wrong attitudes**. It's so easy to get distracted in today's world. The lure of money, success, and materialism can keep you from devoting yourself to your purpose.

I have a friend who was pastoring, and he was a good pastor. He had position, influence, and what most would consider a successful ministry. Yet there was something gnawing at him that he couldn't avoid. He didn't feel pastoring was his purpose. He eventually gave up the pastoral ministry and devoted himself to music. He began writing songs in earnest and today he travels the world, ministering in song and teaching others how to embrace a lifestyle of worship.

Before my friend could come into his purpose, he had to give up a comfortable living as a pastor. Another pastor once told me that he would not leave the pastorate because he would lose his pension. I'm not sure that was an adequate reason to remain.

As I mentioned earlier, you're a hireling if you work for money, no matter what your job. You should work to help establish and strengthen God's Kingdom wherever He sends you. Your provision is His responsibility. He is committed to provide for you in any and every situation.

Don't let money, pride, success, fear, the acclaim of men, or ministry success keep you from fulfilling your purpose. A correct attitude is essential if you are to find your mission. When you find it, take whatever steps are necessary to carry it out.

5. **Don't focus on your purpose at the expense of your relationship with the Lord**. In Acts 13, Saul was finally released to the Gentiles. Acts 13:2 says, "The Holy Spirit said, '*Set apart for me* Barnabas and Saul'"(emphasis added). The Greek phrase "set apart for me" is in the middle voice, which can denote someone doing something to oneself. The middle voice in this verse denotes that the Holy Spirit was calling them to their purpose by calling them to Himself. Your revealed purpose should never take on greater importance than your relationship with the Lord. If it does, God will resist you until your priorities are correct.

Paul understood this and wrote about it to the Philippian church.

> *For to me, to live is Christ and to die is gain. If I am to go on living in the body, this will mean fruitful* [effective] *labor for me. Yet what shall I choose? I do not know! I am torn between the two: I desire to depart and be with Christ, which is better by far; but it is more necessary for you that I remain in the body* (Philippians 1:21-24).

As important as Paul's mission was, he was ready to leave it to be with the Lord, for that was "better." He was content to stay on because it was useful to so many, but he was ready to leave it at any time. That attitude enabled Paul to be even more effective, since his focus was on the Lord and not on ministry or the people.

God doesn't need you. He does, however, choose to use you. Don't take yourself too seriously! After all, God spoke to Balaam through a donkey, and He can get praise from rocks if He so desires. Take God seriously and you'll develop an effective lifestyle. Take yourself too seriously and you'll become busy but not effective.

If you keep an eye out for these roadblocks, your journey on the road to clearly defining your purpose will be a smooth one. In the next chapter, let's look at some more simple steps that will help you write out your purpose statement.

Chapter Six

Steps to Help Define
Your Purpose

We've already looked at Proverbs 25:2, which states, "It is the glory of God to conceal a matter; to search out a matter is the glory of kings." You're a child of God the King, and that makes you royalty. Part of your royal inheritance is to search out the things that God has chosen to conceal.

Richard Bolles writes,

> The puzzle of figuring out what your Mission in life is, will likely take some time. It is not a problem to be solved in a day and a night. It is a learning process which has steps to it, much like the process by which we learned to eat. As a baby we did not tackle adult food right off.[10]

Since discovering your purpose is a process, it is helpful to take the following steps to help clarify your purpose. As it becomes clear, then commit yourself wholeheartedly to pursue it. That's the only way you'll be truly effective.

1. Write down what your purpose is *not*. List those things that you've tried and found no success in doing. Also identify what you had *hoped* your purpose would be, but have found that it is not. Be honest and look at things to which you have devoted yourself that have not borne much fruit.

2. List any things you have done that were easy or seemingly insignificant and for which people have complimented you.

Your purpose can be so natural that you assume everyone sees life like you do or can do what you do so well. That is usually not the case, for your purpose will cause certain things to come naturally to you, but not to most people.

3. Identify verses of Scripture and Bible characters that have meant the most to you. Write them all down and see if there is a pattern. For example, David has always been special to me, because of the price he paid to lead his own people out of chaos into order.

4. Reflect on the earliest words or impressions you had from the Lord, for often they contain clues to your purpose. My earliest impression was a call to "full-time service." I realize today that "full-time" was a clue to the busy nature of my work.

5. Read Covey's book, *The 7 Habits of Highly Effective People*. As I mentioned in the Introduction, Covey is a Mormon and you won't agree with all his "theology," but the book still contains some excellent material. I'm confident you will sort out the good from the bad without throwing out "the baby with the bath water." There is a growing number of books devoted to the topic of purpose. I urge you to make them part of your reading priority.

6. What is it you do that, when you do it, you "feel His pleasure"? What gives you your greatest excitement in life or work? If you have ever suffered from burnout, what did you still have energy to do?

7. Take all this material and work on a purpose statement with a one-sentence summary of your purpose. You will become more and more effective as you endeavor to do what is necessary to fulfill this purpose with excellence.

You may also want to refer to Covey's section on writing a personal mission statement (pages 106-109 and 128-130). To help you further visualize a mission statement, I've included a draft of my own. You may structure yours differently, but I share it with the hope that it will stimulate you to write one from your own understanding and experience.

MY PERSONAL MISSION STATEMENT

I surrendered my life to Jesus Christ on May 18, 1973. The next day I received His call to "give my life to full-time service." From that, I have come to realize that my purpose in life is to "bring administrative order out of chaos wherever the Lord chooses to plant me" using Genesis 1:2 as my guide. To do this effectively I commit myself to:

1. Be a giver and not a taker (Mark 10:45).
2. Produce more than I use (Hebrews 5:11-14).
3. Act according to the will of God and not personal gain (Philippians 2:19-24).
4. Be an example of hard work and diligence (1 Corinthians 15:10).
5. Use my humor as the gift of God that it is (Nehemiah 8:10).
6. Lead with compassion and follow with humility (1 Peter 5:2-4).
7. Continue to study and learn until I die (Psalms 119:18).
8. Walk in faith financially (Hebrews 10:35-39).
9. Be a source of godly wisdom (Proverbs).
10. Invest all I can in the lives of others (1 Thessalonians 5:14).
11. Be an example of order and discipline (1 Corinthians 14:33; 2 Timothy 1:7).
12. Use the Word of God as my guidebook for life and death (2 Timothy 3:16).
13. Help each member of my family to find his or her purpose (Proverbs 22:6).

SECTION TWO

EXCELLENCE: Be Careful Where You Dig

"It is by his deeds that a lad distinguishes himself if his conduct is pure and right."
— Proverbs 20:11 (NAS)

Chapter Seven

Excellence Defined

Once you stake your claim to the field that holds your gold, it's important to begin digging in the correct area. It's not enough to know your purpose and be able to describe it to others. You must begin to achieve excellence around that purpose, which comes in part from setting and achieving goals.

We saw in Section One that the apostles chose to focus on their purpose and not be diverted by "waiting on tables." That allowed them to focus on the first principle we discussed, which was *effectiveness*. The second principle they exemplified was *excellence*, for Acts 6:1-7 tells how the early church grew and prospered under their care. The simple decision to appoint deacons led to better care for the widows, growth in the church, and focused ministry for the apostles. The end result was excellence.

The verse used on the title page for this section (Proverbs 20:11) summarizes the two camps that believers generally fall into when it comes to defining excellence. The first is the "deeds" camp that would express excellence mainly in external things. They would build the finest buildings, publish the best ministry magazines, and produce the most efficient ministry outreaches.

The second is the "conduct" camp. They would point out that modern televangelists got into trouble not because they didn't have external excellence, but because they were missing an internal commitment to excellence that is expressed in holy living.

Unfortunately, both camps fall short of giving an accurate definition of excellence. The "deeds" people have not always been strong on behavior and therefore have sometimes discredited themselves due to moral or integrity failures. In their pursuit of the goal, they often believe that the end justifies the means. On the other hand, the "conduct" people, although living a holy life, have often produced works that were shoddy and unimpressive by anyone's standards

As we begin this section, it's important for us to understand what excellence is and what it isn't. Years ago I set my goal as perfection, equating perfection with excellence. That brought me nothing but frustration, for I could never quite get it all right. No matter how well I planned or how hard I worked, something would go wrong. In time, the Lord helped me to see the difference between *perfection*, which will never be achieved this side of eternity, and *excellence*, which is a heart attitude that produces quality work and conduct.

There are several situations that the Lord used to help me distinguish between perfection and excellence. One such instance was an event I was organizing in my early days as a meeting planner. I had responsibility for a small conference, including the program and publicity. After the program was finalized, I designed the promotional brochure and was ready to mail it when, to my dismay, I saw a misspelled word on the front cover!

The mailing labels were ready; the brochure needed to be in the mail yesterday; and I was confronted with this error that was clearly my fault since I was the only one who had proofed the brochure prior to printing. What was I to do? I was committed to excellence, but a new brochure would cost almost $400 to print, and my deadline was at hand.

I decided to reprint the brochure at my own expense. If it had gone out and I had not noticed the error, that would have been one thing. But the fact that I saw the error meant that I could not just send it out and trust those who saw it to overlook it and forgive my mistake. In this case, my commitment to excellence had to be more than lip service.

Another time I was helping a brother put in a pool deck for another member of our church. When we were planning the job, we estimated how much concrete we would need and then ordered some extra. To our shock, after we had poured what we ordered we were two yards short! When the additional concrete came, it didn't match what had been put in previously.

The pool owner wasn't pleased, but we hoped that he would

overlook the mistake and not make us redo the job. After all, we were brothers in the Lord and friends, and mistakes do happen. He wasn't going to settle for a job that was unsatisfactory, however, and we ended up covering the deck with outdoor carpet at our expense. We were committed to excellence, and that commitment required that the job be finished according to the reasonable expectations of the one who was paying the bill. Asking his forgiveness wasn't an acceptable resolution to a job that had been inadequately completed.

The third instance was when my wife and I reexamined our commitment to excellence as it pertained to having guests in our home. We weren't comfortable with our guests staying in our guest bedroom, which required that they share the bathroom at the far end of the hall with our children. So we decided to stay in the guest room ourselves and let our guests use our bedroom with its attached bath. It was easy to talk about excellence, but because we had a lot of visitors come through our home, it was more difficult to put it into practice.

And finally, my concept of excellence would not be complete without this last story. In 1986, my family and I visited the San Francisco area for a much-needed Christmas vacation. While there, we visited a mall where I purchased four dress shirts on sale at a Nordstrom's department store, well-known for its commitment to excellence. We visited several other stores when I suddenly realized that the bag with the shirts was missing! We retraced our steps and gradually realized that my shirts were nowhere to be found. As a last resort, I went to the counter where I had purchased the shirts and asked if anyone had turned in my bag to them.

Without hesitation, the salesperson told me to pick out four more shirts. I explained that I couldn't afford four more shirts, to which she replied, "You won't have to pay for them!" She enlisted the help of two other employees, who cheerfully found four shirts like the ones that I had misplaced. I was in shock as she handed me the bag and wished me, "Happy New Year from Nordstrom's."

That's the kind of excellence that I want to practice as a follower of Jesus. Jesus' own ministry represents the epitome of excellence, for Mark 7:37 says, "People were overwhelmed with amazement. 'He [Jesus] has done all things well,' they said. 'He even makes the deaf hear and the mute speak.'" Not only did He do the right things at the right time, but He also did them well.

The word translated "well" in that verse is the Greek word, *kalos*, meaning "excellence, so that there is no room for blame." Jesus did what He did with the right heart and motives, and He produced excellence in His ministry. He was representing God, and His attitude and spirit communicated excellence through what He was and did. For Jesus, excellence did start within Him, yet wasn't complete until it found expression in His external actions.

The people in Jesus' day weren't used to a standard of excellence from their religious leaders. They knew that the Pharisees and lawyers taught but didn't always practice the truth. When Jesus came along and didn't just preach healing but also performed it with compassion and without condemnation, they were amazed. The world still tends to be amazed when they see true excellence in the Church.

That word *kalos* is used in several other verses of the New Testament: A man being considered for the office of elder "must manage his own family well [kalos]" (1 Timothy 3:4); "The elders who direct the affairs of the church well [kalos] are worthy of double honor" (1 Timothy 5:17); and "If you really keep the royal law found in Scripture, 'Love your neighbor as yourself,' you are doing right [kalos]" (James 2:8).

There's another Greek word that denotes excellence and that is *arete*. It's found in 2 Peter 1:5, which states, "Now for this very reason also, applying all diligence, in your faith supply *moral excellence* [arete]" (NAS, emphasis added). It simply refers to any particular moral excellence, whether it be honesty, patience, generosity or similar traits. These traits are internal and begin in the heart.

The final verse to consider as we define excellence is found in 3 John v.6: "You will do well [kalos] to send them on their way *in a manner worthy of God*." John was exhorting the brethren to offer excellent hospitality and care for some visiting ministers. He described this excellent care as hospitality *worthy of God*.

For our discussion, therefore, we will define excellence as ***doing all you do from a right heart and in a manner worthy of God***. This definition combines the concepts found in both *kalos* and *arete*, which are both external (actions) and internal (the heart).

Excellence is nothing less than work that is worthy of the God for whom it is done and that comes from a heart motivation of moral excellence that is the direct opposite of pride, arrogance, vanity, or greed.

This definition of excellence, which refers to both an internal and external expression, is what Covey refers to as the "inside-out-side" approach to life:

> The inside-outside approach [to life] says that private victories precede public victories, that making and keeping promises to ourselves precedes making and keeping promises to others. It says it is futile to put personality ahead of character, to try to improve relationships with others before improving ourselves.[1]

Perhaps without knowing it, Covey is indirectly referring to biblical excellence. For him, excellence begins with integrity and then finds expression in the things a person does. Excellence can't be contrived or a fad that a business, ministry, or person decides to pursue. It must be a *lifestyle* that begins in the heart and flows from there into work consistent with that heart condition.

Paul instructed the Colossians concerning excellence when he wrote, "Whatever you do, work at it with all your heart as working for the Lord, not for men, since you know that you will receive an inheritance from the Lord as a reward" (Colossians 3:23-24). Paul wanted them to do everything with a right heart and not just to be noticed by men. But he also wanted them to work hard so that the visible results would give glory to the God who is worthy of all glory.

I have learned that excellence isn't inordinate attention to detail, as I had once thought. Rather it's *a heart attitude that desires to give God the very best in every life situation*. You raise your children with excellence because God cares for His children with excellence. Because God deserves your best efforts, you pursue excellence in your business, home, and ministry. This philosophy causes you to carry out even the smallest tasks with all your heart because you serve the Lord, whose very name is excellent. Out of this heart attitude, you create an atmosphere of excellence where even mistakes can't take away from the finished product because it was done in a manner worthy of God.

In the pursuit of excellence, however, sincerity isn't enough. The fact that you will never achieve perfection doesn't excuse sloppy work. You can be sincere and find yourself sincerely doing the wrong thing or sincerely doing things in a wrong way. You may even have a pure and tender heart toward the Lord and His service, sincerely doing good things for God. But excellence doesn't come from good intentions or being nice. It comes from a concerted effort that will settle for nothing less than the very best in every situation.

Ask yourself: "Am I producing work worthy of God? Does what I'm doing reflect excellence or just my best efforts under the circumstances? Do I settle for good instead of the best?" It's only when you abandon "the good" to give yourself to produce "the best" that you can truly produce excellence and glorify God.

It's a bit surprising that Israel didn't comprehend the issue of ministry excellence, for the Old Testament certainly tried to create the proper mind-set in God's people for it. For example, Moses, David, and Solomon strictly adhered to the building plans God gave them for the tabernacle and the temple that they built using only the best materials. Furthermore, the sacrificial system, decreed by the Law, required that the animals being offered were to be without blemish—the best of the flock. The other offerings for the priests and Levites were to be "all the finest olive oil and all the finest new wine and grain they give the Lord as the firstfruits of their harvest" (Numbers 18:12). In short, the people were taught to give the Lord the best work of their hands.

Jeremiah wrote, "A curse [be] on him who is lax in doing the Lord's work" (Jeremiah 48:10). A "laid-back" attitude in working for God was not to be tolerated. Malachi rebuked the priests for the haphazard manner in which they carried out the work of the Lord:

> "A son honors his father, and a servant his master. If I am a father, where is the honor due me? If I am a master, where is the respect due me?" says the Lord Almighty. "It is you, O priests, who despise my name. But you ask, 'How have we shown contempt for your name?' You place defiled food on my altar. But you ask, 'How have we defiled you?' By saying that the Lord's table is contemptible. When you bring blind animals for sacrifice,

is that not wrong? When you sacrifice crippled or diseased ani-mals, is that not wrong? Try offering them to your governor! Would he be pleased with you?" says the Lord Almighty (Malachi 1:6-8).

Through the prophet, the Lord rebuked His people because they did not strive for excellence. They were approaching the things of God with a mentality of cutting corners instead of asking how they could present the finest service and offerings possible.

Perhaps the most powerful example of excellence in the Old Testament is found in 1 Kings 10:4-9:

When the queen of Sheba saw all the wisdom of Solomon and the palace he had built, the food on his table, the seating of his offi-cials, the attending servants in their robes, his cupbearers, and the burnt offerings he made at the temple of the Lord, she was overwhelmed. She said to the king, "The report I heard in my own country about your achievements and your wisdom is true. But I did not believe these things until I came and saw with my own eyes. Indeed, not even half was told me; in wisdom and wealth you have far exceeded the report I heard. How happy your men must be! How happy your officials, who continually stand before you and hear your wisdom! Praise be to the Lord your God, who has delighted in you and placed you on the throne of Israel. Because of the Lord's eternal love for Israel, he has made you king, to maintain justice and righteousness."

The Queen of Sheba was overwhelmed with Solomon. She be-held not only excellence in action, but a happiness that was equally impressive. This heathen queen broke into praise ("Praise be to the Lord your God") when she described what she had seen. When was the last time anyone began praising God when they described the quality of your work, family, or ministry?

In the tradition of excellent ministry handed down to me by Solomon, Jesus, and many others, I want my brochures, letters, ser-mons, family, and work to represent the excellence of Him who called me out of darkness into His marvelous light. I am not per-fect, nor are the things I work on perfect, but I can pursue excel-lence with all my heart and with a proper attitude.

When I served as a church administrator, I would walk the grounds, inspecting them as I went. When I saw weeds, I pulled them, even though I usually wore a tie. Imagine, weeds were growing on my Father's land! I didn't want delivery people seeing weeds. That may seem extreme to you, and I don't go looking for the weeds of life. If I see them, however, in my sphere of responsibility, I'll pull them because I want excellence.

Gold Nugget Six

"Do you see a man skilled in his work? He will serve before kings; he will not stand before obscure men." —Proverbs 22:29

Martin Luther King captured this spirit when he once said, "If a man is called to be a street sweeper he should sweep streets even as Michelangelo painted, or Beethoven wrote music, or Shakespeare wrote poetry. He should sweep streets so well that all the hosts of heaven and earth will say, 'Here lived a great street sweeper who did his job well.'"

God has put the pursuit of excellence in you. William Temple, who served as Archbishop of Canterbury during World War II, spoke to that fact, saying, "At the root of all your being, your intellectual studies, the games you play, whatever it is, the impulse to do them well is and ought to be understood as being an impulse towards God, the source of all that is excellent." Amen and amen.

Let's now turn to a discussion of how you can pursue excellence on an ongoing basis.

Chapter Eight

A Bull's-Eye on Every Tree

There's an old story of a man who was walking toward a certain town in a day when men walked from town to town. As he was walking, he took notice of targets painted on trees, fence posts, and barns. Each target had a bullet hole exactly in the middle—a bull's-eye on every one. He was impressed with the marksmanship and determined to find and meet this marksman as soon as he reached the town.

When he found him, the first question he asked the man was how had he become such an amazingly accurate shot. To his surprise, the man smiled and told him that he wasn't a marksman at all. He just shot first and then painted the target around wherever his shot landed!

That's how we live when we don't set any goals. Going through life like that so-called marksman doesn't reflect excellence. We shoot first and make it look like we planned where it hit, but that's not the way to excellence. The highway to excellence doesn't involve following the path of least resistance for, as one man said, that "serves only to make both men and rivers crooked." The path of least resistance may make you look good and keep you from failure, but if you aim at nothing, you're sure to hit it. If you set no goals, you can't achieve any measure of excellence.

Let's consider another example, this time from the world of sports. When I lived in Pittsburgh, I was an avid hockey fan. I never played hockey, but I went to as many games as possible. I'd go to the game early because I enjoyed the warm-ups. I watched as the teams came out to skate and check out the ice. The players would skate and shoot the puck at the goalie, who was wearing about 100 pounds of equipment, including big, heavy, leather leggings.

Although I would sit high in the upper-deck seats, I could still clearly hear the big "whap" as the players would hit the goalie on those leggings with their sticks for good luck. All during the warm-ups, they would hit them—whap, whap, whap. As the game approached, the teams would take one final break to go to their locker rooms, only to return to do more "whapping." After the national anthem, the game would begin as the referee dropped the puck for a face-off at center ice.

Now picture in your mind the referee dropping the puck and one of the players passing to his teammate. See that player racing down the ice and shooting the puck at the opposing goalie. Visualize the puck getting past the goalie. The crowd stands, the players look, but alas, the referee forgot to put out the goal net! No one would know whether that shot had reached its goal or not. The game, with all its excitement and pre-game warm-ups, would have no meaning because no one would be able to determine whether that player or the goalie had achieved the goals to which they were dedicated. There would be no excellence achieved for the goalie or the shooter, because there were no set goals.

This hockey scenario reminds me of how it is sometimes in the body of Christ. We have big arenas that seat thousands, and people arrive early to get a good seat. Staff are running around warming up and making a lot of noise, sort of like the "whapping" noise of the players hitting the goalie. We play the game, but seldom know whether we have hit or missed the mark.

We then cover ourselves by saying, "We just want whatever size church God wants; we're not into numbers." We have no goals for Sunday School, the worship team, or finances. We shoot and then paint a target around where the shot landed. There are no goals, and therefore less meaning to the event.

We carry this same mentality into our homes and businesses. Because there are so many variables, we hedge on trying to estimate what our income will be, where we will go on vacation, and how many employees we will have next year at this time. We hesitate to set a goal for furthering our education or getting a new car because we may not make our goal.

Life has meaning when goals are established, and true excellence is achieved only when we set high goals. Without those high goals, you will stay in the comfort zone of life. With goals, you can begin to do "immeasurably more than all we ask or imagine, according to his power that is at work in us" (Ephesians 3:20).

One man who did accomplish "immeasurably more" was George Washington Carver. Carver was an African-American scientist who lived and worked right after the Civil War, perhaps the worst time for a black leader to emerge in the war-torn and racially divided South. Carver was a believer, however, who almost single-handedly improved the lot of the Southern farmer. In a time when his people had few opportunities, he excelled. How was Carver able to do this? He did it by serving his God and setting high goals.

Early in his career, Carver urged farmers to plant peanuts. When the first crop came in, however, there was no market for all those peanuts! Carver was crushed by his sense of failure and naivete. A fictional autobiography of Carver, drawing on true stories from his life, picks up the story from that point:

> I retreated into my lab, only there could I avoid the faces of my students and friends, only there could I be alone. But, somehow I knew I was not alone, even in the silence and stillness, I felt another presence. Falling to my knees, I begged forgiveness from my saviour and creator. And as I prayed, I was drawn to my feet, out of the lab I went into the nearby woodlands and fields. The sun warmed my skin, the soft breezes refreshed my body. "Oh Mr. Creator", I asked softly, "Why did you make this universe?" The winds stirred the trees a bit, "Your little mind asks too much", came the answer. "Ask something more your size." Confused, I rubbed my chin. "What was man made for?" I whispered. Once more I seemed to hear a voice in the wind, "You are still asking too much little man. Try once more." I fell to my knees, "Mr. Creator, why did you make the peanut?" Once more the winds rustled through the trees, "Now you are asking questions your own size. Together, we will find the answers."[2]

George Washington Carver first set a goal of finding as many uses for the peanut as quickly as he could. From his experiments, he discovered more than 300 uses for the peanut. He not only discovered peanut butter and peanut oil, but also found ways to make paper, paint, and paste from that little nut. (In that same lab, Carver later discovered more than 100 uses for the sweet potato.) In a short time, peanut farmers could barely meet the public's demand for their crop!

Carver had set goals that were vague and unattainable, wanting to understand the universe and God Himself. But when he set his sights on a goal within his grasp, with the help of the Lord he found himself on the highway that leads to excellence. Carver changed the world of agriculture because he set a high goal that required God's help.

That's what you need to be doing as a believer! Maybe you are like many other believers who are waiting for someone else to do it. Stop going to the world, but let the world come to you for a change. Find your purpose and begin to set some goals that will make a difference in the world.

Recently, someone gave me a copy of a speech delivered to a group of Alcoa employees by Paul O'Neill, a company vice president. One statement he made caught my attention: "If your calendar is filled up with people who want to see you instead of people you want to see, you haven't got a chance of success."[3]

According to O'Neill, his employees needed to develop their own "action agenda" and stop letting others set it for them if they wanted to be the very best at what they did. He was talking about an action agenda, but he was really talking about setting goals, and then making room for them in the everyday schedule of business.

Covey makes this point so well in his discussion of the first habit of effective people. He calls it "proactivity":

> It [proactivity] means more than merely taking initiative. It means that as human beings, we are responsible for our own lives. Our behavior is a function of our decisions, not our conditions. We can subordinate feelings to values. We have the initiative and responsibility to make things happen.[4]

Six years ago I took a graduate course in systematic theology. I thoroughly enjoyed the course, but it brought me face-to-face with my theological ignorance. I determined to do something about my lack of a ministerial education, even though I had neither the money nor the time.

I set a goal then and there to earn my doctorate within an eight-year period. By so doing, I would graduate when my son graduated from high school. I had no idea where the time and money would come from, but it was something I wanted and needed to do. Furthermore, I believed that the Lord had put this goal in my heart.

I recently received my doctoral degree in pastoral ministry, and have the right to use the designation "Dr. John Stanko." When I first set that goal, a spiritual dynamic was released through my faith. The money has always been there for tuition, and the time to study and write papers has somehow been available.

This same "power" in goal-setting was also made evident to me when my wife and I chaperoned a young adult ski trip to Colorado. I had lived in Pennsylvania all my life, but finally learned to ski (while living in Alabama!) on that ski trip.

On the first day of our stay, a young woman fell and hurt her lower back. She was still in bed three days later when the pastoral team asked me if I would go pray for her. I agreed and found her depressed and in pain as she lay in her bunk. I thought she was down because of her injury, but found out her pain was more than physical.

It turned out that this woman—just in her mid-twenties—had been recently widowed. She didn't want to come on the trip, but her pastor strongly recommended she get away and meet some new friends. She told me that she had come reluctantly but vowed, "When I go, I won't meet any new people." Her goal was not to meet anyone, and at that point in the trip, she had accomplished her goal.

Did she intend to fall and hurt her back? I don't think so. But there was power that was released when she set her goal not to meet anyone. Her goal, as unconscious as it was, set her in a direction that enabled her to achieve it.

I again saw this phenomenon during that same trip when my wife was talking to a group of young people at breakfast. Kathy had learned to ski that week and was discussing getting into a race that required two trips down the mountain. She was sitting next to me and I heard her say, "I just want to make it down the hill one time without falling, and I'll be happy."

I was talking to somebody else at the time, but her comment caught my attention. I intended to tell her that she needed to make it her goal to make it down twice and not just once, but I got sidetracked and then forgot. Later that morning, I arrived at her race site after she had made her first run. If she could match her time in the second run, she would get a silver medal!

I watched in eager anticipation as she began skiing down the hill, only to see her fall just 50 feet down the mountain. She hurt her knee during that fall, and it bothered her for years to come! What happened? I believe that she reached her goal, for her goal was to make one good run down the hill. Just enough power was released for her to do what she determined to do. I'm not talking about a "name-it-and-claim-it" doctrine here, but the book of Proverbs does say, "He who seeks good finds goodwill, but evil comes to him who searches for it" (11:27) and "From the fruit of his lips a man is filled with good things" (12:14).

My doctoral studies have added something to my preaching, this book, and my life in general. If I had only *talked about* getting more schooling or taking a few courses, I would still be ignorant (or less ignorant than I am now). When I set the goal first and then talked about it, the finances, time, and everything else I needed were released. And now there's a new dimension of excellence in my teaching, preaching, and writing that came from my studies. I'm doing a better job because I'm better equipped, leading to a higher degree of ministry excellence.

Gold Nugget Seven

*"All hard work brings a profit, but mere talk
leads only to poverty." —Proverbs 14:23*

Maybe that power to achieve excellence lies in the commitment that you make to do something when a goal is set. W. H. Murray wrote these words about commitment:

Until one is committed there is hesitancy, the chance to draw back, always ineffectiveness. Concerning all acts of initiative there is one elementary truth, the ignorance of which kills countless ideas and splendid plans, that the moment one definitely commits oneself, providence moves too. All sorts of things occur to help one that otherwise would not have occurred. All stream of events issues from the decision, raising in one's favor all manner of unforeseen incidents and meetings and material assistance which no man could dream would come his way. I have learned a deep respect for one of Goethe's couplets:

> Are you in earnest? Seize this very minute.
> Whatever you do or dream you can begin it.
> Boldness has genius, power and magic in it.
> Only engage and then the mind grows heated,
> Begin and the work will be completed.

When you get on the highway to excellence and burn your bridges behind you, the excitement begins. The apostle Paul understood this principle and had a cutting edge in his ministry that helped turn the world upside down. Let's look at Paul and learn how you can release that same dynamic of excellence into your life, work, and ministry.

Chapter Nine

The Anatomy of a Goal

Before we go any further, let's define what a goal is. A goal is *a vision of how it is before it is.* That sounds like something that requires faith, which is the assurance of things unseen (Hebrews 11:1).

While some may view goal setting as being incompatible with spirituality, I see goals as totally consistent, since they require faith. And faith in the Lord always leads to excellent results.

Others claim they are no good at setting goals. Yet I always ask those same people if they pray. When they say that they do, I ask them if a prayer request isn't actually a goal. When you pray, you start out with how it is before it is and pray to see it come to pass. You see someone who doesn't know the Lord and you pray that they will come to know Him; you are visualizing a goal, applying your faith in prayer and working to see it come to pass.

When I tell people this, suddenly they see how comfortable a believer should be in setting goals that require faith in God's great power. And indeed those who achieve a standard of excellence are often those who know how to pray, just as George Washington Carver did.

You could also say that a goal is *an end result to be achieved through dreaming, planning, and diligence.* That process motivates you to begin and keeps you going when things seem to be going poorly. I've often used my imagination to visualize a certain goal, and then tried to figure out an action plan to help me achieve what I "saw." That process has allowed me to stay focused on the end and achieve things that began as just dreams (including this book).

But this is not just a process of self-fulfillment, which Covey and others in the secular world make it out to be. You are created in the image of God, making you an awesome creature. This visualization is not you deciding on your own what you are going to do. This is a cooperative effort between you and the Holy Spirit.

In the Old Testament, Joseph had a vision of his family bowing down before him. He didn't decide one day that he would be the head. The Spirit of the Lord showed that to him. And it cost him quite a lot to see it fulfilled, as we will discuss later.

For further evidence that goal-setting is a spiritual exercise, consider the Apostle Paul. You may think it strange to say that Paul had goals, but he did! He wasn't haphazardly spreading the Gospel. Rather he had a plan with specific strategies to accomplish what he did. Consider these verses written by Paul himself as proof of this point:

> *Therefore I run in such a way as* not without aim [a goal]; *I box in such a way, as not beating the air* (1 Corinthians 9:26 NAS).

> *And thus I* aspired [set a goal] *to preach the gospel, not where Christ was already named, that I might not build upon another man's foundation* (Romans 15:20 NAS).

> *But* the goal *of our instruction is love from a pure heart and a good conscience and a sincere faith* (1 Timothy 1:5 NAS).

> *And for this* purpose [goal] *also I labor, striving according to His power, which mightily works within me* (Colossians 1:29 NAS).

> *Now after these things were finished, Paul* purposed [set a goal] *in the spirit to go to Jerusalem after he had passed through Macedonia* (Acts 19:21 NAS).

It is Philippians 3:14 (NAS), however, that gives the biblical anatomy of a goal: "I press on toward the goal for the prize of the upward call of God in Christ Jesus." That verse shows, first of all, that **a goal introduces tension and opposition**. That's why most people don't like goals. You probably feel like you have more than enough tension and opposition without inviting more.

But Paul "pressed on" and that means that something must

have been pressing against him. Given that fact, Paul had to press through what was pressing against him with greater force if he was going to get anywhere. He understood that a goal would help him do just that.

Jesus must have understood that as well because He "for the joy set before him endured the cross, scorning its shame, and sat down at the right hand of the throne of God" (Hebrews 12:2). The goal for Jesus was the seat at the right hand of God. To get there, He pressed through the Cross and its shame. If a goal did that for Jesus, it will do the same thing for you.

As already mentioned, one goal for me was my doctorate. At times everything in me wanted to watch television, but I knew I had class tapes to watch. At other times, I wanted to buy a *Time* magazine in an airport so I could just do some leisurely reading. I couldn't do that because I had class reading to complete if I was to finish my goal and pursue excellence. There was something pressing against me, and I had to press through it. The goal of my doctorate helped me to do that.

If you already have tension and opposition in your life without goals, why not set some goals of where you want to go? Then the pressure and opposition will have some meaning because they are coming to prevent you from getting where you want to go. Your desire to achieve your goal will give you incentive to overcome it all to succeed.

Second, Philippians 3:14 teaches that **a goal offers a prize**. When you set a goal, two things can happen: You can achieve it or fail trying. In the game of goal setting, there are winners and losers. That's part of life, but too often you can try to play it safe. There's no prize or excellence in living like that. If you set the goal, you may not win; if you don't set the goal, you can't win. There's a big difference.

Next, **a goal is upward**. It brings you closer to God and godliness (if it's truly a godly goal). Again, I draw from my experience of going back to school. My doctoral studies taught me a great deal about the Lord and His Word. That goal was not just academic; it was spiritual. And because it was, it brought me closer to the Lord and gave me greater love for Him, His people, and His Word.

And finally, **a goal involves a call**, a specific task that God has set before you to do. It's my belief that the Lord put the desire for my degree in my heart in the first place. What I accomplished was something that He had set before me to do.

Paul set goals that were prompted by the Spirit, and he helped turn the world upside down with the message of the Gospel. He didn't just run the race any way he chose. He set the course by establishing goals and then ran that course with discipline and purpose. Today many still emulate Paul's method of ministry because it set such a high standard of effectiveness and excellence.

Like Paul, who encountered struggles when he pursued his goals, you too will encounter any number of obstacles standing in your way as you seek to win the prize at the end of your goal.

In some sense, the ball is in your court. You can enjoy the presence and mercy of God, but God doesn't give you those things because He wants you to feel good. God is after something, and you are a part of His plan. Don't receive His grace in vain. Use it rather to set high goals and count on that grace to help you succeed with excellence. With that in mind, let's now turn to a discussion of those things that will work against you achieving your goals and how you can minimize their effect.

Chapter Ten

Your Goals Have Enemies

For the first few years I pastored a small church, we had a terrible sound system. We had a pair of stereo speakers, cheap microphones, and we were content with that for much too long.

The church fasted for three weeks one January, as was our custom. During that fast, I determined (and sensed it was God's will) that it was time for us to get a new and better system, so that became our goal. Shortly thereafter, we heard about a system for sale that had everything we needed. There was only one problem—our lack of money.

The church didn't have any savings, nor did we have many high-income members. Not letting that deter us, we told the man that we would buy his system. I then announced that a special offering would be taken two weeks later. That offering was a miracle. One man just happened to receive a surprise settlement from an insurance company, and he alone paid for half the system. I'm still not sure where the rest of the money came from, but we were able to pay for that system with cash. That goal helped us have better audio quality that contributed to our pursuit of ministry excellence.

Looking back, I can see that I put up with an inadequate sound system for two years because we had a small church, and I didn't believe God could give us anything more. That attitude represents the most formidable enemy working against your goals—**unbelief**. The writer of Hebrews tells us,

> *Who were they who heard and rebelled? Were they not all those Moses led out of Egypt? And with whom was he angry for forty years? Was it not with those who sinned, whose bodies fell in the desert? And to whom did God swear that they would not enter*

his rest if not to those who disobeyed? *So we see that they were not able to enter, because of their* unbelief (Hebrews 3:16-19, emphasis added).

This passage equates unbelief and disobedience. If you're walking in unbelief, you're being disobedient, and that's sin, no matter how you slice it.

We used to rent a house where we kept the trash cans in a small alcove outside the front door. One morning I went out to take the cans to the curb and as I did, I walked into a big spider web. That web acted like a hair net and stuck to my hair like glue. I went back inside and stood in front of mirror to get the web out of my hair and the thought came to me, "That's how unbelief is." You can walk into it and not even realize it until it's too late. It clings to you, and it requires some effort to get it off.

For instance, you may have the thought one day, "I need to learn Spanish." If you're not careful, you will immediately walk into the web of unbelief and think, "No, I can't. I don't have time. Besides, I was not good at languages in school. Maybe when my kids are in college, I'll have time to do it."

Or maybe you have the idea that you want to learn to play the piano. But then the web traps you with thinking like, "Oh, it's too late in life. I don't have the time or patience to practice." The web of unbelief comes on you and sticks to you like glue. You're paralyzed in that web and afraid to move out.

I'll give you another example of what I mean. I once owned a car that began to give me all kinds of trouble. After two or three major breakdowns, I was still determined to be a good steward and not buy another one. The problem was that I found myself witnessing to every tow truck driver within a 50-mile radius of where I lived. I told the Lord, "God, if you want me to witness to these men, please send them to my church and not to pick me up in my broken-down car!" But I was still determined to be a good steward.

Finally, I broke down in Perdido Key, Alabama, and had to be towed more than 85 miles. I had had enough. When I got home, I went to a Dodge dealer and said, "I want a Caravan." The salesman asked, "Which one?" and I responded, "I don't care, just give me your best deal." I signed on the bottom line and drove that van home.

I didn't have the money in my budget for either a down payment or the monthly payment of $429.52. I paid off that car early, however, and it was a tremendous blessing for over 120,000 miles. At first I didn't believe that the Lord could get me a new car. But then I decided that if I could have faith for the old one to run, I could have faith to be able to make the payments on a new one.

You may long for a computer, new musical equipment, or an advanced degree. Is $100 per month keeping you from something that could launch your career or ministry or make your current one more productive? Is that faith? If you are serious about excellence and there is something you need to help you achieve it, are you willing to use your faith to get it? Again, it's easy to talk about excellence but not always comfortable to pursue it.

It's not faith that requires you to know everything from the beginning before you'll step out and do something. It's presumption and pride to insist that the Lord show you everything before you will trust Him and take the first step. Didn't Abraham leave his country not knowing where he was going? Did God explain everything to him before he left? Of course he didn't, and so He commended Abraham for his faith and made him your father in the faith. You are expected to follow in his footsteps.

Now you may think I'm teaching debt here, but I'm not. David described what I'm trying to impart when he wrote,

> *For though the Lord is exalted, yet He regards the lowly; but the haughty He knows from afar. Though I walk in the midst of trouble, Thou wilt revive me; Thou wilt stretch forth Thy hand against the wrath of my enemies, and Thy right hand will save me.* The Lord will accomplish what concerns me; *Thy lovingkindness, O Lord, is everlasting* (Psalm 138:6-9 NAS, emphasis added).

The bottom line is this: Do you believe that the Lord *will accomplish what concerns you*, regardless of how impossible it seems? If you don't, then you're walking in disobedience, because you are commanded to have faith. If you do believe that, then what are you prepared to do about it?

At one time I trusted the Lord for over $2 million in ministry income. I could do that in part because I learned to trust him for a

$429 monthly van payment. We will return to the subject of faith in Section Five, but for now let's end our discussion of unbelief with a poem:

> There's no thrill in easy sailing, when the skies are clear
>   and blue.
> There's no joy in only doing things, which anyone can do.
> But there is some satisfaction that is mighty sweet to take,
> When you reach a destination that you thought you'd
>   never make.
> —*Unknown*

Setting goals in faith will help you go where you thought you never could. It will provide your greatest testimonies of how the Lord helped you to do the impossible as you trusted Him. If you pursue the right goals, they will add to your level of excellence.

The next great enemy of your goals is **low self-esteem**. I respected and utilized principles of inner healing and deliverance in my pastoral counseling, but after 20 years of pastoral ministry, I've come to the conclusion that if you suffer from low self-esteem, you're really in a pretty good place. Now before you panic and accuse me of heresy, let me explain what I mean.

Paul wrote in Romans 7:15, "What I want to do, I do not do," and in verse 18, "I know that nothing good lives in me…for I have the desire to do what is good, but I cannot carry it out." Some think Paul was talking about his life before Christ when he wrote this, while others think he was stating a fact of life that was true even after conversion.

I think Paul was describing his true current condition when he wrote those verses. After all Paul had learned and done, he knew there wasn't anything in him that was "good." The same is true for you, if you'll stop and think about it.

There's nothing in you that you can spit-shine and present to God that will be acceptable in His sight. Thank God that's not the end of the story, for He gave you the Holy Spirit as a down payment of the glory that is yet to come. You didn't receive some portion or expression of the Holy Spirit, but rather the same Holy Spirit that raised a dead man (Jesus) back to life!

If you're feeling like you aren't worth much, you may be right!

There may be no good thing in your flesh. But the Spirit in you has made and is making you into a new creation. Focus your worth on what the Spirit is building in you, and you'll have new vision for what you can accomplish. And you'll realize that your ability to accomplish great things for the Lord doesn't depend on how your father treated you or how your mother changed your diapers!

Paul also wrote in Galatians 2:20 (NKJV), "I have been crucified with Christ, it is no longer I who live but Christ who lives in me, and the life I now live in the flesh, I live by faith in the son of God who loved me and gave himself for me."

Now it may be difficult for you to think of Paul as dead and worthless. He went on to write, "I am the worst [of all sinners]" (1 Timothy 1:15). You may think Paul was just saying that in religious humility, but it was true. Paul was the worst. He was a murderer and thought he was doing God a favor by killing people. In essence, he was saying, "It is no longer I who live but Christ who lives with me, and I'm just as glad. Let Him shine through me and let me be the vessel He works through."

Gold Nugget Eight

"The Lord will be your confidence." —Proverbs 3:26

Paul also explained his ministry in terms of what God was doing in him:

> *I became a servant of this gospel by the gift of God's grace given me through the* working *of his power.... Now to him who is able to do immeasurably more than all we ask or imagine, according to his power that is* at work *within us* (Ephesians 3:7,20, emphasis added).

The phrases "working" and "at work" both come from the Greek word *energeia,* and it's the word from which we derive the word "energy."

There was a divine energy in Paul that came from the Holy Spirit. Will it be any different for you? You won't do great and excellent things for God because you're smart, talented, or gifted. God will use those things, but you'll accomplish your goals through "the grace given through the *working* of his power." Jesus did all things well through the working of that same power.

Paul prayed for the Ephesians that they would know "his incomparably great power for us who believe. That power is like the working of his mighty strength" (Ephesians 1:19). You have power through faith. If you want power to do more with excellence, focus your faith on some high goals. Get your eyes off your inadequacies and on the greatness of the power. God will only do "immeasurably more than all we ask or imagine *according to his power that is at work in us*"(emphasis added). If there's no power working in you, then God can't do the immeasurably more. It's just that simple.

The third enemy you have in goal setting is the **fear of failure**. You can be so paralyzed by the fear of failure that you may not try to do anything at all. This truth came home to me as I was reading the sports section one day. When Pete Rose, former baseball great, was closing in on the record for the most career base hits, an interesting statistic caught my eye. Rose had more than 4,000 hits and had a career batting average of just over .300. That meant that he had come to bat more than 14,000 times. If he had 4,000 hits, that meant he had failed to get a hit more than 10,000 times! For every hit (his goal every time he stepped to the plate), he had 2.5 failures. Yet he was considered a great player until character flaws pulled him down.

Do your past failures or the fear of new ones tend to keep you in the dugout? For fear of striking out, will you not even try to get a hit? Are you so afraid you'll do the wrong thing that you miss opportunities to do the right thing? If you answered "yes" to any or all of those questions, then you have a problem with the fear of failure and you need to face it and get rid of it.

It may help you to realize that mistakes and failures are part of the learning process. You don't discipline a child learning to walk when that child falls down. Because they are learning, you encourage them to keep on trying. Pete Rose wasn't born knowing how to hit a baseball. It's the same with life and with goals, even spiritual ones.

People ask me every now and then how I learned to plan conferences. (This is another aspect of bringing order out of chaos. When I begin planning a conference, there's nothing there; yet order comes from this void when I go to work.) Even though most of my conferences have gone smoothly, I've had my share of failures. Those failures have taught me more than my successes. If that is true, were those "failures" really failures or were they really successes that taught me important principles through difficult circumstances? Even a baseball player may strike out only to learn something about the pitcher that enables him to hit a home run the next time up to the plate. Suddenly his strikeout is not a failure, but a learning experience on the way to a success.

I planned a meeting in Dallas one time that was a disaster. The night before the event, I had a dream that the meeting was a disaster. Slipping into the bathroom at 3 a.m. so as not to awaken my roommate, I actually took notes, listing 14 things that went wrong with the meeting of my dreams.

When I awoke the next morning, I shared the dream with my co-workers. We were expecting 1,200 people, however, and didn't really take the dream too seriously until that evening when only 300 people came. It was a financial and spiritual disaster. It was painful, and I never want to have a meeting like that again. But I lived and learned through it (and you will, too) when you "fail."

And then there's the question that people always ask: "How can I be sure what I want to do is from the Lord?" My response is always the same: "How do you know it isn't?" You must learn to stop making (out of fear of failure and unbelief) the Lord prove that your idea is of Him and ask Him for proof that it isn't.

Take, for example, Proverbs 16:3 in the Amplified Version:

Roll your works upon the Lord—commit and trust them wholly to Him; He will cause your thoughts to be agreeable to His will, *and so shall your plans be established and succeed* (emphasis added).

Isn't one goal of the Spirit to give you the mind of Christ? Can this happen, and you not even realize it? You can have the mind of Christ, and it occurs in a supernaturally natural manner. How do you expect it to happen—with lightening bolts and electric jolts? Stop dismissing your ideas as insignificant; they may be dripping with potential, waiting for you to accept and act on them.

You're still not convinced? Then consider what Luke wrote to open his Gospel: "*It seemed good also to me* to write an orderly account for you, most excellent Theophilus" (Luke 1:3, emphasis added). He didn't write that the Lord led him to write or that five prophets spoke a word for him to write. Rather he wrote, "It seemed good to me." Luke had a good idea that was supernaturally natural.

It was the Holy Spirit who prompted that idea. The result was the word of God in Luke's Gospel! Your ideas and goals that come from having the mind of Christ are the keys to your success as you pursue excellence.

Look at the Holy Spirit-prompted goal that Jonathan set in 1 Samuel 14. King Saul and 600 men were camped "under a pomegranate tree in Migron" (1 Samuel 14:2). They were going through drills every day, acting like an army in every way except one—their enemies held the high places, and Saul wasn't attacking them. He was just playing soldier!

Jonathan, on the other hand, said to his armor-bearer, "Come, let's go over to the Philistine outpost on the other side" (1 Samuel 14:1). That was easier said than done. Jonathan had chosen a tough goal: "On each side of the pass that Jonathan intended to cross to reach the Philistine outpost was a cliff" (1 Samuel 14:4).

Jonathan, however, was unfazed:

> *Jonathan said to his young armor-bearer, "Come, let's go over to the outpost of these uncircumcised fellows. Perhaps the Lord will act in our behalf. Nothing can hinder the Lord from saving, whether by many or by few"* (1 Samuel 14:6).

Jonathan wasn't looking for a way to dismiss his idea. He wasn't asking God to prove it by sending a prophet or some other miraculous means. Jonathan made it easy for the Lord to confirm what he set out to do: "If they say to us, 'Wait there until we come to you,' we will stay where we are and not go up to them. But if they say, 'Come up to us,' we will climb up, because that will be our sign that the Lord has given them into our hands" (1 Samuel 14:9-10). What faith!

If I were the Philistines, I would of course call out to Jonathan to come up. Why should I leave the advantage of my high place? Yet Jonathan chose the natural response of his enemies to confirm his goal. He wasn't looking for a *way out* of the goal he had set, but rather for a *way in*.

While the armies of God were marching around in the valley, Jonathan was scaling the walls of his enemies. Who had the standard of excellence—Saul who was drilling the army in the valley or Jonathan who stepped out and actually brought the victory? Maybe Saul wanted his army to be the best-drilled army around, but that wasn't the key to excellence for an army surrounded by its enemies! Perhaps Jonathan didn't do it as neatly as Saul would have, but he knew how to set a goal that was high and divinely inspired, and he wasn't afraid of failure.

When we discussed the concept of low self-esteem earlier, we saw that there is energy working in you through the Spirit. Second Corinthians 6:1 adds to your understanding of this energy when it refers to you as "God's fellow workers." The Greek word for "fellow workers" is *sunergeia*, from which the word "synergy" is derived. Properly defined, synergy is "the cooperative action of discrete agencies so that the total effect is greater than the sum of the two effects taken independently." Synergy means that one plus one equals three, or five, or ten!

Covey writes that synergy is the sixth habit of effective people. His synergy, however, takes place between people as they interact. While that is an important and probably the most common place where synergy occurs, the synergy Paul described is between you and God! Imagine the power loosed when God is your "fellow worker"!

You plus God equals synergy of the highest order. He could accomplish His purpose without you but has chosen not to. You working with God can do more than just you alone. That working relationship can produce excellence because He who is excellent can reproduce His excellence through what you do.

The Bible teaches, "Five of you will chase a hundred, and a hundred of you will chase ten thousand" (Leviticus 26:8). Without synergy, two should only be able to put 40 to flight. But working together will increase the yield of two people five-fold!

Paul calls you and me God's "fellow workers." Because of who you work with, you should dress and act like God's fellow worker. That fact doesn't depend on how you feel, where you've been, or how many failures you've had. Synergy can still be realized when you give yourself to the purpose and the goals of God.

Shake off the spirit of failure! Someone once said, "God is

playing chess with man; He matches his every move." Move and watch God move with you. Another person said, "No one can ever be a complete failure, for he can then serve as a horrible example for someone else." Even if you fail, someone can point to you and say, "Don't ever grow up to be like that."

The final enemy we will discuss in this chapter is *lack of diligence.* You can easily underestimate what it will take to achieve your goal and sometimes you want to give up. When you say, "Lord, I want to be used by you," the Lord often responds, "Oh, really? Well, just sign this contract." When you study the contract, however, there's nothing on the page. The Lord then says, "Well, just sign it, and I'll fill in the terms later."

Gold Nugget Nine

"A slothful man does not roast his prey, but the precious possession of a man is diligence." —Proverbs 12:27 (NAS)

That is what the Lord did in my own call to ministry. I waited 16 years for a pulpit. I was called to the ministry when I was seven years old; when I met the Lord at age 23, He confirmed my call. Five years later, I moved to Mobile, Alabama, where I preached two times in 11 years! I was one of the youngest men on a 20-man pastoral ministry team. There I was, praying for 19 men ahead of me to "go home" or get transferred so that I could have a chance to minister!

During those long years, however, I used Covey's second habit—begin with the end in mind—to help me prepare myself. I wanted people to remember me as a great preacher (I have a long way to go on that), so I started preparing to be a great preacher. During those 11 years, I planned, prepared, and dreamed for the day when I would get a pulpit.

I would analyze sermons and see what worked and what didn't. I would preach to myself, my kids, the goldfish, my home meeting, and to anybody who would listen. At the same time, the Lord worked some of the character in me that would be needed for the ministry to which I was called. When eventually I went to Orlando to pastor, I was ready because I had been diligent. I will discuss my call to the ministry again in Section Five.

There's even a better example in the Old Testament of what I am trying to communicate. Earlier in this section I mentioned that in the book of Genesis, Joseph had two dreams, both indicating that his family would bow down to him. Let's assume, just for the sake of discussion, that Joseph was 17 years old when he had those dreams. Shortly thereafter, his brothers sold him into slavery. When he arrived in Egypt, Joseph faithfully served as a slave in Potiphar's house. Mrs. Potiphar tried to seduce Joseph, but when he didn't succumb to her advances, she lied and claimed that he tried to seduce her. That landed Joseph in jail.

When he was 30 years old, or about 13 years after his dreams, Joseph was brought before Pharaoh and interpreted Pharaoh's dreams. Pharaoh was so impressed that he promoted Joseph to be his second in command. But the story didn't end there. Joseph needed more diligence.

Joseph then led Egypt through seven years of plenty. By then, he was 37 years old and there was still no sign that his dreams would ever be fulfilled. It wasn't until the second year of the famine (see Genesis 45:6) that Joseph revealed himself to his brothers. Just prior to that, we are told that Joseph "remembered his dreams about them" (Genesis 42:9).

If you have trouble remembering your dreams from last night, how did Joseph manage to keep his dreams alive for at least 22 years? He kept them fresh in his mind by rehearsing them. Even though everything seemed to work against his dreams coming to pass, Joseph was diligent in jail, in Potiphar's house, and as Pharaoh's vice president. Joseph knew how to keep the goal out in front of him! He maintained a standard of excellence no matter what he was doing, and it led to his promotion and the fulfillment of the dreams the Lord had given him.

In the pursuit of excellence, Covey asks his readers to determine what the center of their life is. He lists spouse, family, money, work, possessions, pleasure, friends, enemies, church, and self as the most common centers around which people shape their lives. "By centering our lives on timeless, unchanging principles," he says, "we create a fundamental paradigm of effective living."[5]

But rather than centering your life on principles, I encourage you to center your life on the Lordship of Jesus Christ. Make Him your Lord, the reason and focus for all you do. Only He can impart and define those "timeless, unchanging principles." Only He, through the Holy Spirit, can show you what your purpose is and then reveal what projects and goals you are to pursue. His Lordship can keep you working when others encourage you to abandon the work. It is not in you to do great things, but He is in you, and together you can do great things. Together you can achieve excellence.

Be diligent. Use the time you have now to prepare for the day when you reach your goal. If you'll keep your goal in front of you, regardless of what the circumstances look like, you'll be motivated to produce excellence, even if what you're doing seems totally un-related to the goal you're pursuing.

I urge you to face the enemies of your goals and learn to master them. Deal with the web of unbelief. Shrug off low self-es-teem. Get out of the grandstands and step to the plate, even though you may strike out. And apply the necessary diligence to see what you've started come to a successful conclusion. If you're willing to do all this, then proceed to the next chapter, which will lead you in an exercise to help formulate and write down your goals.

Chapter Eleven

Let's Set Some Goals

As we begin this chapter, let's look at Habakkuk 2:1-5:

I will stand at my watch and station myself on the ramparts; I will look to see what he will say to me, and what answer I am to give to this complaint. Then the Lord replied: "Write down the revelation and make it plain on tablets so that a herald may run with it. For the revelation awaits an appointed time; it speaks of the end and will not prove false. Though it linger, wait for it; it will certainly come and will not delay."

From this passage, you have the basic steps of how to set your own goals. Let's look at it phrase by phrase.

1. **"I will stand at my watch and station myself on the ramparts."** First of all, get away from the phone and all other distractions. Go to the library, a public park, your church sanctuary, or your favorite place of prayer. If you're really serious, you may want to fast and pray before you begin or during the process.

Then "station yourself on the ramparts." Get above the situation in which you're now living. Forget about money (or the lack of it), education, your current job, or the lack of ministry opportunities or career advancements. Remember that "God raised us up with Christ and seated us with him in the heavenly realms in Christ Jesus" (Ephesians 2:6). Take your place with Christ and look down on your life.

Exercising faith that "in his heart a man plans his course, but the Lord determines his steps" (Proverbs 16:9), begin to examine every area of your life. Ask yourself where you want to be and what you would like to accomplish in the next two years in your job, ministry, family, finances, health, and spiritual life. As you formulate goals, ask yourself what you must do to make those goals a reality.

For instance, if you are a pastor and desire to see your church double in size within two years, what is your plan to see that happen? How often will you pray, what will you preach, and who will you enlist to help you reach your goal? If you want to write a book, how many pages per day or week must you write to be done in two years? If you want or need to do more reading, how many books will you read per month and what kind of books will they be?

2. **"I will look to see what he will say to me."** Add to your goals those that may be unexpected or seem out of character for you because they may be from the Lord. You may never have thought of furthering your education, but sense that may be an issue about which the Lord is speaking. If it is, make it a goal. Remember not to dismiss something right away as being ridiculous or far-fetched. Exercise some faith and do something to see if the Lord won't confirm your unexpected thoughts and desires.

Take time also to renew those past dreams that you've abandoned due to family responsibilities, lack of time or money, or discouragement. Let the Lord energize those old "castaways" into active goals once again.

I can't emphasize enough the need for you to take your impressions and thoughts seriously during this process. Don't be so ready to dismiss them as too wild or impossible. See what God will say to you and find a way to do it instead of finding excuses not to.

3. **"Write down the revelation."** Don't just think about your goals; write them down! And don't just write them down on a scrap of paper or a legal pad that can be misplaced easily. Record your goals in something you carry with you everywhere. If you don't use anything like that now, invest in a pocket calendar or notebook to which you can add sheets of paper. The whole idea behind writing down a goal is to keep it visible before you.

In Psalm 50:17, the Lord rebuked His people, "You hate my instruction and cast my words behind you." When you have a goal and you believe it's something that the Lord has put in you to do, don't cast those words behind you. Keep them in front of you. Writing them down helps you do just that. Writing down a goal also helps insure that you take it seriously. Furthermore, it prevents you from abandoning the goal during tough times.

4. **"For the revelation awaits an appointed time."** A goal isn't truly a goal until a time schedule has been worked out for its fulfillment. Once you have answered what you will do, you must then decide when you expect to complete it. Until that happens, a goal still lives in the land of dreams.

As mentioned previously, Nehemiah was asked by his boss, the king, "How long will your journey take, and when will you get back?" Nehemiah responded, "It pleased the king to send me, so I set a time" (Nehemiah 2:6). Nehemiah had not even seen Jerusalem or the scope of the task, but he set a timetable as best he could.

Robert Schuller wrote,

When you set goals, put a time limit on them. Without it you are normally and naturally lazy and lethargic more often than you want to admit. It's amazing how much you can accomplish in a short period of time if the pressure is on. What do you do when you have not succeeded in meeting your time limit, and it becomes apparent that the project will take longer than you expected? You keep walking in faith. You revise your timetable: "It's not impossible, it just takes a little longer." Suddenly seemingly unachievable projects become very realistic! What can you accomplish if you take ten years? You might be able to get a new degree. Perhaps you can acquire a much larger financial base. You might even be able to overcome that handicap. Keep walking the walk of faith. Don't give up believing; just revise the timetable! *God never promised to deliver an answer to prayer according to our timetables* (emphasis added).[6]

Once you have set a time limit, you are ready for the next step...

5. **"Though it lingers, wait for it."** Schuller spoke of the need for flexibility in the above quote, and he's right. Goal setting is not a science but an art. You don't have perfect knowledge, and you can't foresee the unexpected. If you could, you may not set out on your goal's journey at all! You make your best estimates, realizing that you may need more time.

Schuller again writes,

Give God time, and He will perform the miracle. When a human condition appears to be totally impossible, don't check out; ask for an extension of time. The hotel sign reads, "Check-out time is 12:00 noon." Don't believe it if you run into a predicament! Ask and believe. They will extend the check-out time. Just don't get locked into an iron-clad schedule. Don't surrender leadership to a clock or a calendar. Of course you set time-dated goals. Of course you generate energy by creating urgency. But be prepared to revise your timetable before you bury your dream! Every passing hour of every passing day and every new month increase the possibility that things will turn around. What you may need is not more faith, but more patience. The impossible may become possible when you take the long look. As we walk the walk of faith, we must become more God-like. And one quality about God is his immeasurable long-suffering and patient attitude. What great impossible deeds could you accomplish if you had a forty-year goal? If you are tempted to abandon your dream—don't! (emphasis added)[7]

I've found that typically I'll reach about one-third of my goals annually, another third will see some progress, while the final third seem to die shortly after they are set. I try never to discard the latter but re-evaluate them annually and carry some over to the next year.

This book took longer to write and publish than I anticipated. My doctoral studies took a year or two longer than I expected. But

I was further along even with the delays than if I had waited for everything to be perfect before I started.

Before closing this section, there are two other important aspects of goal setting that you need to remember. The first is to **share your goals with someone you trust**. Job 22:28 (NAS) says, "You will also decree a thing and it will be established for you; and light will shine on your ways." Then Malachi 3:16 (NAS) states, "Then those who feared the Lord spoke to one another, and the Lord listened and heard it, and a book of remembrance was written before Him for those who fear the Lord and who esteem His name."

Those two passages attest to the fact that, when you declare your goals, an unseen spiritual dynamic and energy described earlier in this chapter are released. Your commitment to a course of action is sealed when you tell someone, because now they will be free to ask you, "How are you doing with that goal?"

The second and last aspect is to **have courage and act**! Courage is not the absence of fear, but acting in the midst of it. David said to his son, Solomon,

> *Be strong and courageous, and do the work. Do not be afraid or discouraged, for the Lord God, my God, is with you. He will not fail you or forsake you until all the work for the service of the temple of the Lord is finished* (1 Chronicles 28:20).

Let's close by looking at one last verse from the book of Nehemiah, the story of a man who marshalled the people toward a common goal. Nehemiah 6:15 states,

> *So the wall was completed on the twenty-fifth of Elul, in fifty-two days. When all our enemies heard about this, all the surrounding nations were afraid and lost their self-confidence, because they realized that this work had been done with the help of our God.*

Commit to do something great for the Lord, see it through to the end, do it with excellence, and then watch God's enemies be disheartened.

Now that you have begun to set goals, the next section will

help you manage your time so that your goals can find a place in your already busy schedule.

SECTION THREE

EFFICIENCY: Don't Settle for Fool's Gold

"One who is slack in his work is brother to one who destroys."
—Proverbs 18:9

Chapter Twelve

What a Timeless Book Says About Time

A recent issue of *Bits and Pieces* magazine contained this challenging quote from Susan Ertz: "Millions long for immortality who do not know what to do with themselves on a rainy Sunday afternoon."[1] This quote perfectly describes some people I know. They mean well and have a lot of vision, but they waste time and never seem to live up to their full potential. What's more, God's purpose suffers with them as they waste the most precious commodity of all—their time.

A while back, I came across an issue of *Christian History* magazine that focused entirely on the life and ministry of Charles Haddon Spurgeon, the great 19th century British preacher and author. Two pages were devoted to unusual facts about this productive man and his ministry, some of which pertain directly to our study of time management. Consider these facts about Spurgeon:

•*The New Park Street Pulpit and The Metropolitan Tabernacle Pulpit*—the collected sermons of Spurgeon during his ministry with that congregation—fill 63 volumes. The sermons' 20-25 million words are equivalent to the 27 volumes of the ninth edition of the *Encyclopedia Britannica*. The series stands as the largest set of books by a single author in the history of Christianity.

•Spurgeon typically read six books per week and could remember what he had read—and where—even years later.

• During his lifetime, Spurgeon is estimated to have preached to 10,000,000 people.

• Spurgeon spent 20 years studying the book of Psalms and writing his commentary on them, *The Treasury of David.*

• By accepting some of his many invitations to speak, Spurgeon often preached 10 times in a week.

• Spurgeon often worked 18 hours a day. Famous explorer and missionary David Livingstone once asked him, "How do you manage to do two men's work in a single day?" Spurgeon replied, "You have forgotten that there are two of us."[2]

Spurgeon was a gifted man and minister, yet he also knew how to manage his time and get the most out of every day. Who wouldn't want to leave the legacy that he did, but who is willing to pay the price that he did?

I have subtitled this section "Don't Settle for Fool's Gold" because I'm fascinated by the California gold rush of the 1850s. During that time, people from all over the world sold all their possessions and travelled to California, often with only the clothes on their back, to search for personal fortune. Some found it, and others gave their lives in a futile search.

Imagine someone paying the price to come to California and then one day discovering a shiny object in the ground. Assuming it to be gold, they staked their claim only to find that they sold all they had not for gold, but for something that only looked like it— fool's gold.

That's how it can be with you. You can be busy and fill each day with well-intentioned activity. You can work hard and collapse in exhaustion each night. At the end of the day, however, you may only have fool's gold to show for your work because you wasted your time working on activities that did not represent the best use of your time.

The writer of Ecclesiastes put it this way: "If the ax is dull and its edge unsharpened, more strength is needed but skill will bring success" (Ecclesiastes 10:10). Poor time management is like chopping wood with a dull ax; eventually you can get the job done, but it takes a lot more energy than it does if you use a sharp ax. Becoming skillful at using the resource of time helps you find the real gold you are after, and that gold is functioning in your purpose while working on your goals as we discussed in Sections One and Two.

Before we discuss how to sharpen your axe, let's take a quick look at some of what the Bible teaches about time.

1. Joshua 10:9-14

After an all-night march from Gilgal, Joshua took them by surprise. The Lord threw them into confusion before Israel, who defeated them in a great victory at Gibeon. Israel pursued them along the road going up to Beth Horon and cut them down all the way to Azekah and Makkedah. As they fled before Israel on the road down from Beth Horon to Azekah, the Lord hurled large hailstones down on them from the sky, and more of them died from the hailstones than were killed by the swords of the Israelites. On the day the Lord gave the Amorites over to Israel, Joshua said to the Lord in the presence of Israel:

'O sun, stand still over Gibeon,
O moon, over the Valley of Aijalon,'
So the sun stood still and the moon stopped,
till the nation avenged itself on its enemies,

as it is written in the Book of Jashar. The sun stopped in the middle of the sky and delayed going down about a full day. There has never been a day like it before or since, a day when the Lord listened to a man. Surely the Lord was fighting for Israel!

Joshua needed more time to do the task that was before him. He and his army marched all night without sleep, yet the Lord strengthened the people to fight the next day. Then, when Joshua couldn't finish the battle, he prayed for the sun to stand still, and it did for a full day. So Joshua and his men stayed up for a second consecutive night to finish the job. I know how tired I can be after only a few hours sleep, but Joshua and his men were up for 72 hours and could still function!

Some commentators interpret the sun standing still to mean that the Lord actually "froze" the sun in the same position for almost a day. Others believe that somehow the Lord empowered the people to fight, and they were able to accomplish much in an unusually short period of time; for them, it means that the sun only *seemed* to stand still.

Whatever happened, Joshua trusted the Lord for more time, and he got it. Because Joshua knew what the real gold was, he efficiently used the time he had and then exercised faith for the extra time he needed to do the job. He refused to settle for fool's gold.

I'm sure that you're learning to trust the Lord for finances, necessary changes in your heart, and ministry or career opportunities. But you must also learn to trust him for time, for He is Lord even over your time. He can do miraculous things for you just as He did for Joshua.

2. Ecclesiastes 3:1-8

There is a time for everything,
and a season for every activity under heaven:
a time to be born and a time to die,
a time to plant and a time to uproot,
a time to kill and a time to heal,
a time to tear down and a time to build,
a time to weep and a time to laugh,
a time to mourn and a time to dance,
a time to scatter stones and a time to gather them,
a time to embrace and a time to refrain,
a time to search and a time to give up,
a time to keep and a time to throw away,
a time to tear and a time to mend,
a time to be silent and a time to speak,
a time to love and a time to hate,
a time for war and a time for peace.

There once was a time when I read that passage and wondered, "How can I know for sure what time and season it is? How can I know when to tear down or build? Speak or be silent? Search or give up searching?"

Gold Nugget Ten

"He who gathers crops in summer is a wise son, but he who sleeps during harvest is a disgraceful son." —Proverbs 10:5

The answers to those questions couldn't be found in a system with rules of what to do and how to do it in every situation. There were simply too many options before me every day to try to follow a set of rules. I began to find my answers to those questions first in 1 Chronicles 12:32, which describes the men of Issachar as those "who understood the times and knew what Israel should do."

The sons of Issachar, like Joshua before them, knew what they should do. They knew that it was the season to install David as king, and they gave their time to accomplish that task. If they knew where to invest their time, I determined that I could, too. Yet how did they know for sure?

That led me to John 7:17, which states, "If anyone chooses to do God's will, he will find out." That told me if I would commit to do God's will in every situation before I knew what it was, He would show me what His will was for my life and my time. Finally, I read that "those who are led by the Spirit of God are sons of God" (Romans 8:14), and my answer was complete. Since I was a son of God, His Spirit would lead me if I was committed to do God's will, whatever it was.

And that's the basic secret to good time management. The Spirit is able to help you sort out your priorities and lead you in the way you should spend your time. There can never be one set of rules to govern every situation that will come your way; on one day it will be time to build, and on the next it will be time to tear down. Only the Spirit can show you what needs to be done, and then only you can decide to spend your time on what the Spirit directs you to do.

3. Proverbs 3:1-2

"Keep my commands in your heart, for they will prolong your life many years."

Most time management systems try to squeeze more time from every day, and some even promise to help you find two hours or more per day. But better organization isn't the way to get more time. Obedience to God's will is the only way you can really get more time.

Gold Nugget Eleven

"For through me your days will be many,
and years will be added to your life." —Proverbs 9:11

If you obey what the Spirit directs you to do, your obedience will extend your years and expand the amount of time you have available. That's what happened to Joshua, and it will happen to you.

There are many times when I have had a lot to do. Yet when I have followed the Lord's will for my time, He has supernaturally given me more time to catch up with things. There were times when I spent time with my son even though I had a report to work on. There were other times when I gave up what I was working on to obey my supervisor's request for an urgent item. There were times when I prayed even though I had an early meeting for which I hadn't prepared. In each case, the Lord helped me with the time I had left because I trusted Him by obeying His will for the time I had. He truly can prolong the days of your life if you keep His commands in your heart.

4. 2 Peter 3:8

Another important aspect of time for you to understand is that God is seldom in a hurry, nor is He ever late. The Lord isn't committed to our concept of time, but expects us to walk according to His perspective. Peter gave us some important insight when he wrote, "But do not forget this one thing, dear friends: With the Lord a day is like a thousand years, and a thousand years are like a day." I always thought that sounded so spiritual until one day I did some simple math and came up with a better understanding.

If you divide 24 hours into 1,000 years, you can see that each hour with the Lord is the equivalent of 42 years; if you divide 60 minutes into 42 years, each minute is like 8.5 months; if you divide 60 seconds into 8.5 months, you see that every second to the Lord is like four days! So if the Lord tells you He'll be there in a minute, you may have to wait more than eight months!

Isaiah wrote, "Those who wait for the Lord will gain new strength" (Isaiah 40:31 NAS). My time management can never circumvent the fact that the Lord is in control. I can't make anything happen unless it's in His time; the harder I try, the more frustrated I can become. There are some things that just have to wait, and I can't do anything about it.

5. Ephesians 5:15-16

This verse is worth looking at in several different translations. It says, *"Be careful then how you live…*
…making the very most of the time" (AMP).
…make the most of every opportunity to do good" (LB).
…making the most of your time" (NAS).
…make the best possible use of your time" (Phillips).

Paul urged the Ephesians to make the most of their time, and that exhortation applies to you today. There's only one way to make the most of your time, and that's to spend it on activities that will bring the greatest return for the Lord and His Kingdom. Don't take a trip and just stare out the window for hours; don't spend a good part of your day in front of the television set. Don't settle for fool's gold, but use your time to go after the most important issues—the real gold—that are worthy of your efforts.

Covey refers to the real gold in life as "Quadrant II" activities—activities that are not urgent but important.

Quadrant II is the heart of effective personal management…. It deals with things like building relationships, writing a personal mission statement, long-range planning, exercising, preventive maintenance, preparation— all those things we know we need to do, but somehow seldom get around to doing, because they aren't urgent. To paraphrase Peter Drucker, effective people are not problem-minded; they're opportunity-minded. They feed opportunities and starve problems. They think preventively.[3]

The Lord expects you to be not a victim of time that slipped away, but one who redeems the time. If you could free up 15 minutes every day for one year to read the Bible, for example, at the end of the year you would have read the equivalent of 3.8 full days! Begin to seize those moments that you have wasted away. Over a period of time they will add up.

6. Proverbs 18:9

Before we close, there's just one more point to make. If you don't do something that needs to be done, you have acted just like someone who took what was done and undid it! Proverbs 18:9 is the verse on the title page for this section. It states, "One who is slack in his work is brother to one who destroys." Your inability to do the important things is the same thing as getting them done and then tearing them apart. If you build a shed and then burn it down or don't build the shed in the first place, isn't the end result the same?

If you miss an opportunity that God has given you, you're related to one who would destroy. You may think, "It's no big deal; nobody got hurt because I didn't learn Spanish," or "Nobody suffered because I didn't start that business." That may be true, but you don't really know what would have happened had you started and completed it.

If you feel some pressure reading that statement, that's good. Paul urged the Corinthians "not to receive God's grace in vain" (2 Corinthians 6:1). If he warned not to do that, then it must be possible to receive God's grace in such a way that the Lord gets no return on His investment. God's grace has come, but He has work for you to do. So roll up your sleeves and let's look at some principles that will help you achieve efficiency through better time management.

Chapter Thirteen

How To Be a Wise Guy

Time is the great equalizer. You may not have as much talent or money as others, but you have as many hours in the day as they do. You have the same opportunity as they to maximize your efforts so that, at the end of the day, you can know you did the things the Lord put before you to do.

Before we go on, let's define the term "efficiency" to mean **the ability to get supernatural results using limited human, financial, and physical resources.** Joshua was an efficient general and used his limited time and fighting men to win the battle. Gideon routed the Midianites not with the 32,000 men with which he started, but with the 200 men who survived the tests of bravery and watchfulness. Jesus took five loaves and two fish and fed 5,000 people with plenty of leftovers. Paul, in a matter of a few decades, had planted enough regional churches to reach most of the known world.

A popular saying goes, "If you want something done, ask a busy person to do it." It seems as if those who manage their time well can almost always fit something else in. When someone approaches me about a job or a request for help, I try to find how I *can* do it instead of how I *can't*. In addition to the verses discussed in the previous chapter, I've studied three other biblical principles that have helped me tremendously in my quest for efficiency and good time management. They are **wisdom, stewardship,** and **dominion.**

Wisdom

Let's begin by defining wisdom as **the ability to use knowledge in a supernatural manner.** You need wisdom on a daily basis if you are going to manage your time well. Just having the knowledge of what to do is no guarantee that you have the know-how to apply that knowledge; that comes only through wisdom.

Every day you're faced with so many things you can do and need to do. But you're also faced with many interruptions, and you have limited resources. On top of all that, you have pressures against you such as depression, fatigue, doubt, and fear. These things try to keep you from being productive and all that God wants you to be. Given those realities, you need wisdom. To move from *knowing* what to do to actually *doing* it requires wisdom.

Wisdom isn't some sage sitting cross-legged with his disciples gathered around him as he pontificates, nor is it a system of beliefs, new ideas, or philosophies as the ancient Greeks supposed. Wisdom for you and me is a *person*—our Lord Jesus Christ. Paul wrote to the Colossians about this Christ, "in whom are hidden all the treasures of wisdom and knowledge" (Colossians 2:3) and to the Corinthians about Christ, "the power of God and the wisdom of God" (1 Corinthians 1:24). Paul understood clearly that our wisdom was a man, not a concept.

That's why a set of rules can't possibly cover every time management situation that you will face. The carnal or religious man (as opposed to the spiritual man) craves a system because when he has a system, he no longer has to rely on the Lord. If you had a foolproof guide of how to plan every day in every way, you would carry on in your own understanding without any need for the Lord's input. But you have need of wisdom and that comes from a vital relationship with a living God who is able to communicate clearly to you in every situation. Your efficiency will come from a living word from a living God that will energize you to do more with less because He is strengthening you to do it.

It's interesting what Solomon asked for when he became king. He didn't actually ask for wisdom to rule, but for a "discerning [understanding] heart" (1 Kings 3:9). He wanted to be able to hear what the Lord was directing him to do. Because he didn't ask for money or the death of his enemies, the Lord granted his prayer.

God gave Solomon wisdom and very great insight, and a breadth of understanding as measureless as the sand on the seashore. Solomon's wisdom was greater than the wisdom of all the men of the East, and greater than all the wisdom of Egypt. He was wiser than any other man....And his fame spread to all the surrounding nations. He spoke three thousand proverbs and his songs numbered a thousand and five. He described plant life, from the cedar of Lebanon to the hyssop that grows out of walls. He also taught about animals and birds, reptiles and fish. Men of all nations came to listen to Solomon's wisdom, sent by all the kings of the world, who had heard of his wisdom (1 Kings 4:29-34).

You might say that Solomon was efficient, writing songs, poems, riddles, and exploring the glories of God's creation. He took his limited resources and added them to God's limitless resources. The results were awesome!

You need that same listening heart. One problem you will encounter as you listen, however, is that there are many voices vying for your attention. Proverbs 9 depicts both Wisdom and Folly sitting on the high places of the city and "calling out to those who pass by" (Proverbs 9:15). When you pray, do you suddenly think of all kinds of things that you have to do? When you prepare to work at your desk, in your shop, or at the kitchen counter, do projects other than the one before you cry out for your attention? Because Solomon realized his propensity to be overwhelmed by these urgent voices to do so many things, he asked for a listening heart so he could manage his time and life well.

You, too, should ask for wisdom to know how to use your time and energies. And when you do, the Lord will say to you what He said to Solomon:

Since you have asked for this and not for long life or wealth for yourself, nor have asked for the death of your enemies but for discernment in administering justice, I will do what you have asked. I will give you a wise and discerning heart (1 Kings 3:11-12).

So wisdom is neither a set of beliefs nor is it a teaching. Godly wisdom is best expressed by *someone creatively doing new things in new ways.* A system requires that you follow what someone else has developed for their world. But that system may not fit into your world because the Lord has put something before you that's unique. I want to face new challenges and find new solutions, perhaps combining old techniques in some new manner. I want to do things that haven't been done and not merely replicate what's already been done.

Proverbs 8 captures the essence of this creative wisdom:

> *The Lord brought me forth as the first of his works, before his deeds of old; I was appointed from eternity, from the beginning, before the world began. When there were no oceans, I was given birth, when there were no springs abounding with water; before the mountains were settled in place, before the hills, I was given birth, before he made the earth or his fields or any of the dust of the world. I was there when he set the heavens in place, when he marked out the horizon on the face of the deep, when he established the clouds above and fixed securely the fountains of the deep, when he gave the sea its boundary so the waters would not overstep his command, and when he marked out the foundations of the earth. Then I was the craftsman at his side. I was filled with delight day after day, rejoicing always in his presence, rejoicing in his whole world and delighting in mankind* (verses 22-31).

The Lord used wisdom to create the world. There was no book He could refer to in order to do it right the first time. Proverbs 8 tells us that wisdom was His guide, the same wisdom that's available to you. If every day in your life presents new situations you've never faced before, then only wisdom will help you work them out. And since you know that wisdom is a person, then you know that Proverbs 8 is actually Jesus speaking. The wisdom that leads to efficiency involves learning how to listen and then having the confidence that you can apply what you've heard to a new and unique situation.

Gold Nugget Twelve

"By wisdom the Lord laid the earth's foundations, by understanding he set the heavens in place." —Proverbs 3:19

Wisdom that leads to a creative solution or efficient use of resources always produces awe for the sovereignty and power of God. Solomon's first test after he asked for wisdom was the case of the two women and the baby. One woman claimed the baby was hers, and the other claimed she was lying. What was Solomon to do? He couldn't ask his father, nor did he have a law library close at hand. So he told them to cut the baby in half with a sword and give half to each woman. The real mother said to give the baby to the other woman. Based on her response, Solomon awarded her the baby. Where did he get that idea from? Solomon was listening, and it resulted in true justice for the real mother. "When all Israel heard the verdict the king had given, they held the king in awe, because they saw that he had wisdom from God to administer justice" (1 Kings 3:28). I want people to hold the Lord in awe because I have wisdom to efficiently run my world and responsibilities.

There are four ways that you can get this divine wisdom. First of all, **you seek it** like Solomon did. Proverbs 2:4-6 says,

> *If you look for it* [wisdom] *as for silver and search for it* [wisdom] *as for hidden treasure, then you will understand the fear of the Lord and find the knowledge of God. For the Lord gives wisdom; and from his mouth come knowledge and understanding.*

Imagine that someone gave you a guarantee that there was a gold bar buried in your backyard. Would you stop searching for it just because you didn't find it after you dug one hole? You would probably dig up your entire yard until you did find it.

That's the urgency and diligence you must apply if you're going to find godly wisdom. You have a guarantee that it's there, but you must seek it. When Nebuchadnezzar gave the order for all the wise men in Babylon to be killed, Daniel sought the Lord for wisdom and received the interpretation to an unknown dream. He got the wisdom he needed because he desperately sought it, and his life depended on finding it.

During a recent transition in my life, I fasted 21 days because I needed the wisdom of God. I was desperate to find the wisdom and understanding that the Lord has promised. You don't find God's wisdom by praying "now-I-lay-me-down-to-sleep" prayers. You find it by paying a price, the same price that even Jesus had to pay. The writer of Hebrews painted a fantastic picture of Jesus' prayer life when he wrote,

During the days of Jesus' life on earth, he offered up prayers and petitions with loud cries and tears to the one who could save him from death, and he was heard because of his reverent submission. Although he was a son, he learned obedience from what he suffered and, once made perfect, he became the source of eternal salvation for all who obey him (Hebrews 5:7-10).

Jesus prayed with a loud voice and tearful cries. He didn't use King James' English and address His Father with religious "Thee's" and "Thou's." He cried out and received what He asked for. If that's the pattern that Jesus used, will you be heard with any less? Jesus was heard not because He was God; He was heard because He paid the price to be heard.

After you seek wisdom, the next step is to **learn to listen to the Spirit who is speaking**. As Jesus was about to choose His 12 apostles, Luke wrote,

One of those days Jesus went out to a mountainside to pray, and spent the night praying to God. *When morning came, he called his disciples to him and chose twelve of them, whom he also designated apostles* (Luke 6:12-13, emphasis added).

Jesus lost a night's sleep praying and listening; afterward, He chose 12 men to be "apostles," something that had no religious precedent. He did something new with God's wisdom and dug deep to find it. Those 12 men, representing a new way of doing things, turned the world upside down. Godly wisdom will help turn your world upside down as well, if you learn to listen and discern what the Lord is saying.

Now you may be concerned about how you will know if the Lord is speaking to you. The only guarantee is found in Hebrews 11:6, where you're told, "Without faith it is impossible to please God, because anyone who comes to him must believe that he exists and that he rewards those who earnestly seek him." If you diligently seek Him, He will make Himself known somehow. It may be through someone else, circumstances, or a small still voice, but He will make Himself known and heard. Your faith will always be rewarded.

The first step is seeking and the next step is listening. The third step to obtain wisdom is to **study the book of Proverbs**. Early in my Christian walk, someone told me to read one chapter from Proverbs every day. Since there were 31 chapters and most months have 31 days, it would then be possible to finish the entire book in one month. I did this faithfully but found I wasn't gaining much ground in retaining what the book had to say.

It seemed that most chapters just jumped from topic to topic with no common theme. A typical chapter would talk about righteousness, speech, finances, leadership, family, and fools. One day I realized that the book was written that way on purpose so the casual reader would not get much out of it. If I was going to understand Proverbs, I knew I would have to do a lot more work than just read it once a day.

So I started to identify seven major themes of Proverbs and placed each verse in the category where it belonged. When I got my first computer, I categorized each verse so that at any time I could reference what Proverbs had to say about money or leadership quickly and efficiently. As a pastor, I began to do all my marital counseling out of the book of Proverbs.

I took the time to study that book and haven't stopped. I've tried to dig out the nuggets of gold contained in every chapter and make them part of my life and behavior. While all Scripture gives wisdom, none but Proverbs was written with that express purpose:

> For attaining wisdom *and discipline; for understanding words of insight; for acquiring a disciplined and prudent life, doing what is right and just and fair; for giving prudence to the simple, knowledge and discretion to the young*—let the wise listen and add to their learning, *and let the discerning get guidance* (Proverbs 1:2-5, emphasis added).

If you need wisdom in your life, then you need the book of Proverbs more than ever before. It was written with the goal of giving you wisdom, but it won't come easily. You will have to dig, study, and read. But to those who pay the price, Proverbs holds priceless gems of wisdom that can make the difference between success and failure.

The final way to get wisdom is to **walk with the wise**. "He who walks with the wise grows wise, but a companion of fools suffers harm" (Proverbs 13:20). I've tried to make it a habit of finding wise men and women of God and walking as close to them as possible. My marriage and children are better for it, and my ministry is as well.

The "me-and-Jesus" mentality so prevalent in the modern believer wasn't the mentality in the early Church. They ministered and functioned in teams and learned to draw on one another's strengths. Learning only from your own experience isn't the best teacher. Learning from others' experiences, especially their mistakes, is a better and more efficient way. And you can do that by following them closely.

If you're disorganized or don't manage your time well, the best thing you can do is find people who are organized and spend time with them. Let them give you some balance and another perspective of how to do things. If you can't walk with the wise, you can at least read their literature. My goal is to read two books every month—one with theological content and one with management principles. And I try to read authors who have been successful in their field, not those who have an idea that *should* work but remains untested. Remember, wisdom isn't just ideas, but someone creatively applying knowledge that God gives to do new things. I want to learn from those who have experience so that I can be equipped to do what is now before me. If you know you need more wisdom than you have now, pray this prayer:

Lord, I need wisdom. I don't use my time as well as I could or should. I need Your wisdom so I can be more efficient. From now on, I will ask You for more wisdom and then listen and watch for Your reply; I will more diligently study the book of Proverbs and I will make every effort to walk with the wise, through relationships, books, conferences, or other media. Help me, Lord. Your Word says, "If any of you lacks wisdom, he should ask God who gives generously to all without finding fault, and it will be given to him. But when he asks, he must believe and not doubt" (James 1:5-6). I'm asking You now, believing that You will give me the wisdom I need according to Your promise. Thank You for hearing me, Lord. Amen.

And now that you're on your way toward getting wisdom, let's study the next concept that will lead to a more efficient life.

Chapter Fourteen

The Butler Did It

Every once in a while, I hear a song that has meant a great deal to me in my walk with the Lord. The words are:

I'm not my own, I belong to Jesus.
Purchased of God, I'm all His.
Bought with a price, the blood of Jesus.
I'm not my own, I'm His.
—*Author Unknown*

It is an awesome realization that you and I belong to Jesus, including all that we have and are. If that concept is true, then your time belongs to Him and you must learn to "spend" it wisely and according to His will. In other words, you must be a good steward over your time.

Our society has lost any concept of stewardship that it may have once had. *Webster's 1828 Dictionary of the English Language* defines a steward as "a man employed in great families to manage the domestic concerns, superintend the other servants, collect the rents or income, and keep the accounts." That sounds a lot like a butler, a position that has all but disappeared from today's list of occupations.

Yet there was a time in my life when I was called to be just such a steward. When I moved to Mobile, Alabama, the Lord joined me to a man of God. Joseph Garlington is a brother whom God has used in ministry around the world. He's my pastor and spiritual father and has trained and discipled me over the years. What has made this relationship special is that Joseph is black and I am white. When I first joined him, I thought I would travel with him and learn to minister as he did. I did do some of that, but the Lord joined me to him so that I could serve his needs while he traveled in ministry.

I cared for his house and finances. I oversaw repairs, paid the bills, purchased chemicals for his pool, sorted his mail and stamped his envelopes. I made sure his cars were maintained and the yard work was done. I took him to the airport and picked him up as he returned to town. There were times when my wife and I moved into his home to care for his children when he and his wife were on the road for an extended period of time.

This may seem a bit unusual, but the Lord was using this relationship to do something in my life. First, he was dealing with my ambition and pride (which were all too abundant). Beyond that, the Lord gave me what belonged to someone else and had me manage it efficiently and carefully. During this season, my time was not my own. It had to be organized according to Joseph's needs and schedule. As I learned that, I saw the reality of that same principle in my life and work—my time and work opportunities belonged to the Lord and I had to submit my will to His as to how they would be used and spent.

I studied God's Word during this training time and found that I was following in the footsteps of **Jacob**, who cared for Laban's sheep; of **Joseph**, who cared for Potiphar's house and the needs of his fellow inmates; of **Moses**, who tended his father-in-law Jethro's flocks; of **Joshua**, who was Moses' servant; of **David**, who watched over his father's sheep; and of **Elisha**, who would "pour water on the hands of Elijah" (2 Kings 3:11).

The Lord prepared each of those men for ministry by having them be a steward for a period of time. When I saw that pattern, I embraced what I was doing and tried to learn all I could about being a good steward. I admit there were times when I cried out to the Lord, hoping there was more for me than what I was doing then. But for several years, that was the path the Lord had chosen to develop my ministry.

I had to learn to care for someone else's world just as I would care for my own. I came to realize what Jacob meant when he said to Laban, "I did not bring you animals torn by wild beasts; I bore the loss myself. And you demanded payment from me for whatever was stolen by day or night" (Genesis 31:39). As a steward,

Jacob was responsible for what went on. If there was loss or if a predator ate one of the flock, Jacob paid for it out of his own pocket.

Jacob understood, and I came to understand, that a steward wasn't supposed to just maintain the status quo. He was there to keep watch and bring increase, as Jesus also pointed out:

> The Lord answered, "Who then is the faithful and wise manager [steward], whom the master puts in charge of his servants to give them their food allowance at the proper time? It will be good for that servant whom the master finds doing so when he returns. I tell you the truth, he will put him in charge of all his possessions. But suppose the servant says to himself, 'My master is taking a long time in coming,' and he then begins to beat the menservants and maidservants and to eat and drink and get drunk. The master of that servant will come on a day when he does not expect him and at an hour he is not aware of. He will cut him to pieces and assign him a place with the unbelievers" (Luke 12:42-46).

A steward was expected to work efficiently without oversight to carry out the will of the master. If he did so, he would be promoted. If he did not, then he would be in trouble with the master. The Lord wanted me to learn this lesson practically because it is such an important principle in life, work, and ministry. If I couldn't prove myself faithful with Joseph's world, how could the Lord give me my own? But if I managed my time and opportunities successfully, I would be a good steward, fit for Him to use and promote.

Gold Nugget Thirteen

"Like a bad tooth or a lame foot is reliance on the unfaithful in times of trouble." —Proverbs 25:19

Peter instructed the early Church, "As each one has received a special gift, employ it in serving one another, as good stewards of the manifold grace of God" (1 Peter 4:10 NAS). If I had gifts, they were to be used not as I wanted, but according to the will of the one who gave them to me. My time, which was given to me by the Lord, was to be used according to His wishes and not my own.

Today I have a much freer hand to manage my own time because during that period of my life I used my time as a good steward to serve someone else. I surrendered my dreams and goals to those of another as the Lord directed me. I brought order and increase in another's world, and now the Lord has given me my own world.

Stewardship isn't a job with a job description; that belongs to a hireling. Effective stewardship isn't achieved by the master describing what he wants. Stewardship is a heart matter. It involves the heart of the steward being joined to the heart of the master in such a way that communication takes place without words. It allows the steward to operate like the master would want in situations where the master has not laid down specific guidelines of what to do. Let me again explain this by means of another biblical example.

When Naaman the Syrian was healed of his leprosy, "Naaman and all his attendants went back to the man of God [Elisha]. He stood before him and said, 'Now I know that there is no God in all the world except in Israel. Please accept now a gift from your servant.' The prophet [Elisha] answered, 'As surely as the Lord lives, whom I serve, I will not accept a thing'" (2 Kings 5:15-16).

Elisha had a steward named Gehazi who must have been close by and heard what Elisha said to Naaman. The story continues, however, for "after Naaman had traveled some distance, Gehazi, the servant of Elisha the man of God, said to himself, 'My master was too easy on Naaman, this Aramean, by not accepting from him what he brought. As surely as the Lord lives, I will run after him and get something from him'" (2 Kings 5:19-20).

Gehazi did so, and Naaman was only too glad to give Gehazi two talents of silver and two sets of clothing. Gehazi had two of his own servants carry all this home, at which point he took the gifts and put them away in his own house. But when he met Elisha again, Gehazi was in for quite a shock:

"Where have you been, Gehazi?" Elisha asked. "Your servant didn't go anywhere," Gehazi answered. But Elisha said to him, "Was not my spirit [heart] with you when the man got down

from his chariot to meet you? Is this the time to take money, or to accept clothes, olive groves, vineyards, flocks, herds, or menservants and maidservants? Naaman's leprosy will cling to you and to your descendants forever." Then Gehazi went from Elisha's presence and he was leprous, as white as snow (2 Kings 5: 25-27).

Gehazi failed to realize that stewardship is a heart matter. He thought that he could operate according to what *he* thought was best. After all, he felt that his master had missed a chance to obtain a nice contribution for the ministry. Perhaps Gehazi felt justified in taking a little something because a steward's salary wasn't that much. His independence while he was a steward was his undoing, and it caused him and his descendants much trouble.

I want my heart to be joined to my Master's in such a way that I can do what I do with His heart. I want to use my time the way He wants me to use it. As a good steward, I desire to represent Him well by being punctual and making the most of the opportunities that He has given me. I want to hear Him when He says it's time to take clothes and silver, and I want to be willing to carry that out. In the same spirit, I want to know that it's time for me to write a book and use my time as a good steward to do just that.

I learned that principle by caring for my pastor and tending his ministry during my formative years. When I was young in the Lord and eager to carry out my own ministry agenda, I learned to put my agenda aside to serve the interests of another. When I did that, it gave me insight on how to do the same thing for the Lord.

Paul wrote the Philippians,

I have no one else like him [Timothy], *who takes a genuine interest in your welfare. For everyone looks out for his own interests, not those of Jesus Christ. But you know that Timothy has proved himself, because as a son with his father he has served with me in the work of the gospel* (Philippians 2:20-22).

At one time, I prayed that I could be a Timothy to some Paul. What I really meant was that I wanted a Paul who could advance my ministry career. I learned over the years, however, that a real Timothy is a good steward, serving as a son would serve his father. Furthermore, a real Timothy learns to care for something the way someone else wants it done and not the way he wants to do it.

You're to be a steward regardless of whether you think of it in those terms or not. You aren't free to watch a football game, sleep, socialize, or pursue a hobby solely because you want to do it. You aren't free to resign your job or ministry position because you don't like the way you're being treated. You must learn to steward your time and opportunities, seeing them as a loan from the Lord. Your time is a valuable resource—perhaps the most valuable that you have—and you must manage it, find ways to increase and stretch it, so that you will be able to give an account of how you used it as a good steward.

While being a good steward requires many characteristics such as diligence, faithfulness, loyalty, and commitment, perhaps the most important is faith. The servants who invested their talents in the parable found in Matthew 25 had faith that allowed them to risk their investment in order to bring an increase.

Abraham's servant in Genesis 24 also exercised faith as a steward. Abraham enlisted his servant's help in finding his son, Isaac, a wife. Having taken an oath that he would not find Isaac a wife from among the Canaanites, the servant set off for Abraham's homeland in search of Isaac's bride. Abraham must have had great trust in his servant to assign him such an important task. But from the servant's perspective, it must have been quite a challenge. How would he know where to go and who the right woman was?

This steward was a man of faith, however, and that's probably why Abraham chose him in the first place. The steward wanted to do an efficient job of finding the right person, so he prayed the kind of prayer that only a steward with faith can pray:

O Lord, God of my master Abraham, give me success today, and show kindness to my master Abraham. See I am standing beside this spring, and the daughters of the townspeople are coming out to draw water. May it be that when I say to a girl, "Please let down your jar that I may have a drink," and she says, "Drink, and I'll water your your camels too"—let her be the one you have chosen for your servant Isaac. By this I will know that you have shown kindness to my master" (Genesis 24:12-14).

This man was given an almost impossible task to do, but he turned it into an efficient operation. He prayed, sat down, and trusted the Lord to answer his prayer. The results were instantaneous! "Before he had finished praying, Rebekah came out with her jar on her shoulder" (Genesis 24:15). The servant asked her for water, and she offered water for his camels. By faith he knew that this was the girl for his master's son. He returned with Rebekah and Isaac was delighted, "so she became his wife, and he loved her" (Genesis 24:67).

I want to be a good steward like that. I not only want my heart joined to my Master's, but I also want Him to choose me for difficult tasks. And then I want to use my faith to make those jobs time-effective and efficient, just like Abraham's servant. Abraham's servant could have spent months or years finding the right woman, but instead did it in the least amount of time possible.

That kind of efficiency takes more than a good system or well-maintained calendar. You must be trained to have the mind of a steward, seeing every moment as a gift from the Lord. Those moments are precious and should be used in ways that will glorify the Lord. It takes faith and wisdom to be a good steward. When you have been trained as a steward, you're ready for the next step that will bring the greatest return on the time that you have. Let's turn to that next step now.

Chapter Fifteen

Being Part of the Royal Family

American culture loves to watch the royal family in England. Although their members have fallen on hard times as of late, we still follow their movements with interest. Perhaps every girl has dreamed of having the wedding of a princess, and each boy has wondered what it would be like to be so rich and famous.

Yet the royal family has tremendous pressures to endure. They must be educated and then trained in the finer points of diplomacy and protocol. Not one prince or princess is born knowing how to be "royal." Each one is prepared and reinforced for the rigors of royalty.

The same holds true for those in God's royal family. You must undergo training for your role as a prince or princess. The more you will be used, the more rigorous the training.

I've explained how I served my pastor for a number of years as his steward, but today I no longer have that kind of relationship with him. My stewardship and service in those early years paved the way for a much different relationship today as I have entered new levels of responsibility.

The disciples went through a similar transition with Jesus. Just prior to His death, He said to them,

> You are my friends if you do what I command. I no longer call you servants, because a servant does not know his master's business. Instead, I have called you friends, for everything that I learned from my Father I have made known to you. You did not choose me, but I chose you and appointed you to go and bear fruit—fruit that will last (John 15:14-16).

The disciples' service and stewardship paved the way for a deeper relationship with their Master, and it prepared them to rule the early Church. This new relationship was no longer to be Jesus telling them what to do. Rather He shared His heart with them so that they would "know His business." This information would allow them to bear fruit that would remain. You and I are testimony to the fact that the apostles bore fruit that remains to this day.

This is the transition from *stewardship* to *dominion*. Webster defines dominion as "the power to govern and control and the power to direct, control, use, and dispose of at pleasure." Perhaps the best example of biblical dominion is Adam exercising dominion in the Garden of Eden when he named the animals. He was not just tending the garden; he was ruling it at his discretion.

You need to be trained as a steward because you, too, are to participate in the dominion mandate that was given to Adam. Like your father, you are to "be fruitful and increase in number; fill the earth and subdue it. Rule over the fish of the sea and the birds of the air and over every living creature that moves on the ground" (Genesis 1:28).

Dominion is God's goal for His people. When Peter was confronted with two liars named Ananias and Sapphira, he discerned their wickedness and exercised dominion over the church—and they perished for their lies. That's dominion. When Paul was being followed by a girl with an evil spirit, he turned and cast the spirit out of the girl. That's dominion. When the apostle John condemned those in his first epistle who opposed his teaching, he was exercising dominion.

But dominion isn't only exercised by those in ministry positions. David killed lions and bears while he watched his father's flock. As he began his reign, Solomon practiced dominion as he ruled concerning the two women and the baby. Daniel exercised dominion as he functioned in Babylon for decades.

There will always be an element of stewardship in your dominion, because you're doing all you do under the Lordship of Christ, which is ultimate and pervasive. But that doesn't diminish the fact that "whatever you bind on earth will be bound in heaven, and whatever you loose on earth will be loosed in heaven" (Matthew 18:18). That isn't an exercise for the immature or power hungry. Only those who have been trained in wisdom and as stewards have the right to share in the dominion God has prepared for His people.

One day you will rule with Christ! In fact, you're to begin that rulership in this lifetime. Paul wrote, "God raised us up with Christ and seated us with him in the heavenly realms in Christ Jesus" (Ephesians 2:6). That has implications now as well as in the age to come.

Let me say that I hope the next age is more than singing. Now don't get mad at me. I like to sing, but I can't imagine that all the preparation in this life is for one eternal song service in the next. The implication from some of the Lord's parables is that those who rule well now will rule even more in the age to come. John wrote, "You have made them to be a kingdom and priests to serve our God, and they will reign on the earth" (Revelation 5:10).

In his book *The Biblical Doctrine of Heaven*, Wilbur Moorehead Smith expanded on this when he wrote,

> Thus we may safely say, as many have, that there will be a number of activities in heaven which will be a continuation of our labor for Christ here on earth, without, of course, exhaustion, weariness or failure....It is work as free from care and toil and fatigue as is the wing-stroke of the jubilant lark when it soars into the sunlight of a fresh, clear day and, spontaneously and for self-relief, pours out its thrilling carol. Work up there is a matter of self-relief, as well as a matter of obedience to the ruling will of God. It is work according to one's tastes and delight and ability. If tastes vary there, if abilities vary there, then occupations will vary there.[4]

The beauty of this is that God's people will be rewarded according to their faithfulness, if not in this life, then in the life to come. You now should have renewed vision of why it's so important to rule your time, learning to use it effectively. You are a prince or princess in training, preparing for the throne that is yours. If you can't be on time for an appointment, how will you rule a city? If you can't use your time to write your book, learn French, get your degree, or plant a vegetable garden with your children, how will you be able to enter into the dominion mandate that will certainly require hard work and faithful service?

Time management does prepare us for the next age, but it also brings benefits in this life, not the least of which is *peace*. Have you suddenly awakened at 2:00 a.m. remembering something you forgot to do for the next morning? Have you ever promised to return a call but forgot? Did you ever pull an "all-nighter" because you neglected to study or write the paper until the last minute? Would you describe those feelings as peaceful? If anything, they produced stress and anxiety. Too many of those situations can actually lead to illness.

When Solomon brought efficient order to his kingdom, "he ruled over all the kingdoms west of the River, from Tiphsah to Gaza, and had *peace* on all sides" (1 Kings 4:24, emphasis added). Everyone under Solomon's reign knew their jobs and performed them. The result was peace, both in and outside his kingdom.

The Lord instructed Moses,

Make linen undergarments as a covering for the body, reaching from the waist to the thigh. Aaron and his sons must wear them whenever they enter the Tent of Meeting or approach the altar to minister in the Holy Place, so that they will not incur guilt and die (Exodus 28:42-43).

The Lord later told Ezekiel,

When they [the priests] *enter the gates of the inner court, they are to wear linen clothes; they must not wear any woolen garment while ministering at the gates of the inner court or inside the temple. They are to wear linen turbans on their heads and linen undergarments around their waists. They must not wear anything that makes them perspire* (Ezekiel 44:17-18).

The servants of the Lord are to be dignified, not running about in a sweat trying to carry out their duties. At the same time they are to cover themselves in the Lord's service. Thus the priests were told to wear linen and not wool garments. Clothing yourself with efficiency will allow you to carry out your duties with a minimum of perspiration, the symbol of human toil. And it will allow you to be dignified, not running around in confusion or always running late.

The curse for lack of efficiency is not only a lack of peace but also bureaucracy. That's right, bureaucracy. Proverbs 12:24 says, "Diligent hands will rule, but laziness ends in slave labor." When you don't progress towards dominion, two things happen. Either things won't get done, or someone will have to be assigned to oversee you so that things will get done. And then someone will be assigned to oversee them and on and on. That leads to bureaucracy.

I don't know of anything I hate more than bureaucracy, layers of management that require time to wade through until someone decides that someone else can or can't do something. I want to rule my world so that I don't need anyone checking up on me. I want to give my word that I will have the report done on Tuesday, and then get it done or communicate in advance that I can't do it.

I also want my staff to operate independently and efficiently—to have dominion over their own spheres of responsibility—so they can make decisions on the spot. If I communicate our objectives clearly and give them authority to act as responsible adults, they won't need a bureaucratic safety net, saving time, and they will serve people with efficiency and effectiveness. That also brings a measure of dominion to the organizations I'm called to lead.

Those who lack diligence will be put to forced labor. Someone must stand over them with a stick or stopwatch to make sure they do the job. I want people who can rule themselves and who understand wisdom, stewardship and dominion. I want that myself, so I endeavor to manage my time well. In this manner, the Lord won't have to assign someone to baby-sit me to see that I do what needs to be done.

Your goal should be dominion, which will require self-discipline and commitment. If you are ready to use your time more efficiently, then proceed to the next chapter where we will discuss some simple steps to help you do just that.

Chapter Sixteen

The Two-Minute Warning

In professional football, the clock stops two minutes before the end of each half. Some teams seem to come alive with that warning. They may have taken their time and plodded along for 28 minutes, but suddenly, in those last two minutes, they become the epitome of efficiency and production. Having rehearsed those two minutes in practice over and over again, the best teams have snatched victory from the jaws of defeat because they knew what to do after the two-minute warning.

What if the Lord gave you a two-minute warning? In fact, He has already done so! As stated earlier, time is the great equalizer among men. You may not have the talent, money, background, or experience of the next person, but you do have the same amount of time in the day. If you live to normal life expectancy, you will have about 26,000 days in which to get an education, raise a family, find your purpose, and carry out the will of God.

The clock is running and you may be in your two-minute warning. The question is: How many days of those 26,000 do you have left? Will you plod along as you have, or will you go without a huddle and produce yardage in the days you have left?

Our society has many phrases that pertain to time, but they are not always accurate. For instance, we say, "It will save time." You can't save time because the clock is always ticking. You can do something more quickly or efficiently and do it in less time, but that time you "save" must be spent on something.

Then we say, "Time flies," but time goes at the same rate for everyone. For those with no plan, however, it can fly by without the desired accomplishments ever coming to fruition. Someone else may say, "I need more time." But there is no more time; 24 hours is all you get. The question may come, "Where has the time gone?" The time has gone where it always goes. Sir Walter Scott understood that time is the measure and value of life when he wrote,

> Dost thou love life?
> Then do not squander time,
> For that's the stuff life's made of.

Not only is time the measure of life, it is also the great equalizer. Alec MacKenzie in his classic book, *The Time Trap,* shares this insight:

> *"I just didn't have enough time."* Yes you did. You had all the time there is. You had the same twenty-four hours, the same 1,440 minutes, that everyone else did. What you didn't have are the skills of managing the time that's available to you.[5]

Then time, its rate of passage, and the amount you have aren't the problems. The problem is *you* and how you use or don't use the time you have. Again MacKenzie states,

> Thus, the very notion of time management is a misnomer. For we cannot manage time. We can only manage *ourselves* in relation to time. We cannot control how much time we have; we can only control how we use it. We cannot choose *whether* to spend it, but only how. Once we've wasted time, it's gone—and it cannot be replaced.[6]

If you can face that fact, then you're on your way to a more efficient lifestyle that will enable you to correct problems that stand between you and your goals.

Identifying how you spend your time involves a process similar to finding how you spend your money. If you were in debt, your problem would be spending more money than you are earning. To get a handle on this, you would determine what your real income is, what your expenses are, and then find ways to either increase your income or decrease your expenses. You would sit down and go over your checkbook, deposit slips, and credit card statements to determine what your assets and liabilities were. Then you would make a budget to structure your spending.

Keeping a time log or inventory is the same first step you must take to become more efficient. Recently, I kept a time log for two days of my week (that log is included at the end of this chapter with a blank sample sheet). When I did my analysis, I found that I had spent four hours watching television! If you would have told me I had watched that much television, I would have flatly denied it. But the analysis wasn't lying.

You may not have as good an idea of where your time goes as you might think. You may want to begin your log by making your best estimates of how you think you are spending your time. At the end of the two weeks, compare what you thought with the reality of what you did. If you're like most people, your original estimates won't even be close. Until you spend a two-week period keeping track of what you've done and how much time it took, you won't know what adjustments to make.

MacKenzie explains the need for a time log:

> A detailed time inventory is necessary, because the painful task of changing our habits requires more conviction than we can build from learning about the experience of others. We need the incentive that comes from seeing the amazing revelations of the great portions of time we ourselves are wasting. There is simply no other way to get the information we need.[7]

Peter Drucker in his book *The Effective Executive* devotes one entire chapter, entitled "Know Thy Time," to the need and procedure to keep a time log. It was here that I was first introduced to this practice. Although Drucker's target audience is the executive, his insights on time, delegation, and eliminating time wasters are must reading for everyone. I try to read this book once a year, and it challenges me every time I read it.

My time log, however, didn't reveal only problems. I was pleased to find that I was spending almost 10 percent of my time in long-range planning. My time log also showed that I was minimizing my interruptions and giving myself to the highest priority work that would produce the greatest long-term results. Finally, it showed that I was properly allocating my mornings and afternoons between "thinking" projects and busy work.

After you have compiled a similar time log and had a chance to review the results, the next step to better time management is identifying a time management organizing system. There are several excellent systems on the market, and I don't recommend one over the other. I personally use the Franklin Covey™ classic size, two-page per day system. But Day Runner™, Daytimer™ and several other companies have adequate systems as well. A computer planner or Palm Pilot™ may be effective if you use it regularly and take it with you most places you go.

The important thing is that you find a system and *use* it. Ask others what they use and take a look at how their system is set up so that you won't have to buy every system you want to investigate. The important thing isn't the system, but that you stop taking notes or making to-do lists on legal tablets or in spiral notebooks. When you need to find or record something, those tablets or notebooks are seldom handy. When that happens, you start another one and before long, you have a pile of notebooks with no idea of what is where.

Your system should include a 12-month calendar and note pages for every day or week, according to your needs. It should be something that you can add pages to as well. If it's computer software, those components are probably part of the operating system.

Once you have found a system that is right for you, you're ready to identify your biggest time wasters. This will require honesty and some reflection as you analyze your log because the answers may not be pleasant or flattering. Only by facing how much television I was watching could I make the decision to stop watching that much. In my experience, the following are the **most common time wasters** you will encounter.

1. **No priorities or written "to do" lists.** You may wonder how this can be a time waster, and the top one at that. Without a to-do list that's properly prioritized, however, you'll be tempted to give yourself to those things you can readily remember, those that you like to do, or those that can be easily done (that make you feel like

you're *really* productive). Being busy doesn't mean you're not wasting time! As we discussed earlier, giving yourself to the wrong thing (fool's gold) is as bad as doing nothing at all. Also a to-do list helps you handle the inevitable interruptions that will certainly come your way.

When people ask me how I accomplish all that I do, I say without reservation that it's my ability to make lists, prioritize those lists, and stick to my priorities. I compose a to-do list for almost every day of the year, including weekends. That may sound legalistic or unrealistic to you, but that's the only way I can wade through my days staying focused without forgetting important things. And as I tell some people, you won't fully appreciate that until you ask me to do something that's important to you. When you see me write it down, you'll know that it has a good chance of being completed.

Writing things down that I need to do isn't being in bondage to my calendar and projects; it's freedom! Having it down on paper frees me to concentrate on the project before me without distraction. It also assures me that if (or should I say *when*) I get interrupted, I can refer back to my list and resume doing what I was doing before the interruption came.

I prepare each day's list either the night before or in the morning and I include prayer, reading, and exercise. When I first began to make a daily list, I would include only those things that I was afraid I would forget. But I found out that those things I didn't include (such as prayer and reading) didn't get the attention they needed because they weren't before me as I planned my entire day. So now they're on every list.

If there's a day when I don't pray or read, I have those items before me. When I do something else, it forces me to make a choice between what I'm doing and prayer. I have to ask myself, "Is this project more pressing than prayer at this point in the day?" There have been times, when confronted with that question, that I have neglected the other activity to pray as I should have earlier in the day.

When I'm on a plane and think of something that needs to be done, I write it down. I turn to the day when I think I will be able to attend to it and record that thought. Then I regularly review past lists to see if any tasks have not been addressed or completed.

Once I make my list, the next step is to *prioritize* that list; again,

I do this every day for every list I have. That's the hardest part of every list. This forces me to make decisions, tough decisions, about where I'm going to invest my time. Remember, we defined efficiency as getting supernatural results using limited financial, physical, and human resources. Setting and following your priorities will lead you to spend time where it matters most and brings the greatest return.

Again MacKenzie gives us additional insight as he writes,

> The key to successful time management is doing the most important task first, and giving it your full concentration, to the exclusion of everything else. The significance of the daily plan is that it forces you to do exactly that. This is planning at its core: Set priorities for the day, and then do the first one first. And that means *first*. Not after checking the mail, not after reading the daily paper, not after clearing away small jobs.[8]

There's no feeling like putting your head on the pillow at night and knowing that, in the midst of interruptions and some activities that were beyond your control, you were still able to give yourself to the highest priority items on your list. You may have spent time with your family, practiced your instrument, or written four pages of your book. I can't say what your priorities should be; I can only exhort and instruct you how to set and follow them.

A well-done list allows you a great deal of flexibility, and that's a hard concept for some to grasp. For instance, my office door is always open to my staff and to most visitors. I can be flexible and handle a lot of interruptions because I have my day written down. When interrupted, I can consult my list and return to the activity when the interruption passes. Or if the day is gone and that item wasn't completed because of too many interruptions or unexpected delays, it's written down and I can consider where to assign it so that I can start it again on another day.

Covey writes in *7 Habits*,

> Because you aren't omniscient, you can't always know in advance what is truly important. As carefully as you organize the week, there will always be times when, as a

principle-centered person, you will need to subordinate your schedule to a higher value. Because you are principle-centered, you can do that with an inner sense of peace.[9]

One more thing about recording and ordering your to-do list: To do this effectively, you must learn to view your life wholistically. Don't include just work or ministry-related tasks, but include personal goals, household repairs, and family needs and activities on your daily list as well. It takes too much energy for me to keep my life compartmentalized. I view every day as one day, and I try to allow my day to flow instead of being chopped up into segments.

When I wrote down only work-related items, I would give my home less attention than it deserved. For instance, my wife would ask me to fix something on Monday, and I would tell her I would get to it over the weekend. I wouldn't write it down, however, and would suddenly remember on Sunday evening that I hadn't done what she asked. I got around this by writing things down that were personal as well as business—and all in one place instead of keeping separate lists for home, family, ministry, and office. Many days have a combination of those items, and they all get evaluated against one another as to which ones will get the highest priorities.

2. **Not setting time limits and deadlines for various steps through a project.** Many people say to me that they work better under pressure, so they wait until the last minute to do something. I admit that I admire their faith, for by waiting until the last minute, they assume that there will be no glitches to prevent them from finishing the task. But ultimately, it's an excuse for lack of self-discipline, and it increases the anxiety level of those who must work with them as they are forced to wait for the finished product. I have also noticed a higher than average sickness level among such people, probably brought on by the stress they introduce through this process.

It's true that many people do their best work when they're under pressure. The pressure allows them to focus all their resources and energies on the task before them. But if these same people can begin to impose self-made deadlines, they will find their efficiency increasing because they're creating urgency around more projects (and allowing more time for unexpected complications).

MacKenzie addresses this tendency by saying,

> Nobody works better under pressure; what really happens is you do the best you can under the circumstances. Usually this is nothing but a subconscious rationale for procrastinating. If you put off a major task until the last minute, with the excuse that you work better under pressure, you leave yourself no time to do the planning that would produce superior results. You also leave no room for correcting mistakes, locating missing information, or incorporating better ideas that might come to you too late to be included. You get the job done, and you may feel like a hero, but the truth is that the work was just good enough, not "better." By not managing your time, you deny yourself the opportunity to do outstanding work.[10]

It's a proven phenomenon that the projects before you tend to fill your day. If you have 20 files to complete, it seems to take as long as if you have three. If that is true, the key is for you to increase the projects before you so that your focused energies will help you to maximize your available time.

Let me explain further. When I began my studies for a master's degree, I determined to finish the degree in five years. To do that, I had to complete one course every two months. No one put that deadline on me; I set it myself. When I received my course work, I would immediately set a plan in motion to be done in two months or less. That meant that every day found "classwork" on my to-do list. I made classwork an urgent item, and my time seemed to expand so I could get that work in.

You may face a project so big that you neglect starting it because you can't see where the end will come. If you begin to devote one hour per day to that project, you'll begin to see the size of the work diminish. You'll have more hope that it can indeed be done and finish the task that once seemed so huge.

3. **Interruptions**. While there are many unavoidable interruptions in almost every day, there are many that can be prevented

with a little planning. Your time inventory should help you identify those interruptions that can be avoided or curtailed. For instance, your inventory may help you see that staff social visits in your office are taking up 45 minutes a day. That's not acceptable and should be attacked as a time waster. Or perhaps you spend a lot of time on the phone talking to people who call you. Setting a certain time in your day when you'll receive and return phone calls can help you cut down on your phone conversations.

As previously mentioned, I keep my office door open. There are times, however, when I continue to work when someone comes in. I listen as they talk, and then determine: 1) if they need my undivided attention, 2) if I can continue working and listening, or 3) if we can re-schedule the talk for another time. I don't always open my mail when it is brought to my office either, and I don't allow mail to accumulate on my desk while I'm gone. Opening and filing the mail doesn't have to be done the exact minute I return or when it's delivered. That's an interruption I try to avoid.

It's also important to know what time of the day is your prime time when you do your best work. For me, my prime hours are in the morning. I therefore schedule my interviews, phone calls, meetings, and work that takes less thought for the afternoon hours. I then try to do my writing in the evening, treating it as a reward for a job well done during the day. Whenever you work best, try to limit interruptions in your prime time!

Don't be distracted by what I refer to as the "call of the wild." You can be praying, reading, or working, and suddenly your mind begins to race with all kinds of thoughts, ideas, and projects. Don't give in to their cries for attention. Instead, write them down on your to-do list, and they'll suddenly stop "calling." If you begin to work on one project and another project sitting on your desk calls out to you, ignore it or stick it in a drawer or closet. That will shut it up and allow you to avoid the potential interruption over which you have control.

4. **Procrastination.** Most procrastination is just plain laziness. It reminds me of the story of the man who went to see the doctor. After the examination, he told the doctor, "Give it to me straight, doc. What's wrong with me?"

The doctor replied, "You have ergophobia."

"It's OK, doc," the man replied, "you can tell me exactly what it is," to which the doctor responded, "It means you're lazy."

Without hesitation, the man said, "Give me that other word again, doc. I have to go home and tell my wife."

The book of Proverbs doesn't use the word *procrastination*. Instead it uses the word *sluggard* 14 times. You learned to procrastinate and you can unlearn it by calling it what it is and then setting some goals and activities with self-imposed deadlines.

Gold Nugget Fourteen

"How long will you lie there, you sluggard? When will you get up from your sleep? A little sleep, a little slumber, a little folding of the hands to rest—and poverty will come on you like a bandit."
— Proverbs 6:9-11

There are a variety of reasons that you may procrastinate, and many of them have to do with fear. You may fear making a commitment, a firm decision, or a mistake, so you postpone making any decision to act as long as possible. Or you may choose to always do easy or pleasant tasks before all others, thus postponing indefinitely those tasks that require the most time and energy. You may also be lazy, forgetful, or lack self-discipline, all of which will keep you from the job at hand. The good news is that all of these problems can be corrected. The bad news is that you must *want* to deal with them and that your basic problem, procrastination, may hinder you from dealing with procrastination.

There is what I call creative procrastination, however, and I encourage you to exercise it when the need arises. If you're faced with an activity that you aren't sure how to start or if you should start at all, then let it rest for a while on an old to-do list. Chances are when you look at it again, you'll have a better idea of what to do and maybe will decide to drop it altogether.

5. **Anxiety**. I qualify anxiety as a time waster because it almost always motivates you to do the wrong thing. Paul wrote to be anxious for nothing because anxiety creates stress, and stress causes you to be less productive and blurs your judgment of what you really should be doing. Remember, doing the right or wrong thing at

the wrong time is actually a time waster because that time could have been devoted to a higher-priority item.

You can be overly anxious so you spend more time double-checking something than is necessary. Anxiety about a test can cause you to spend more time studying than is actually needed. Anxiety gets your priorities out of whack and therefore has the potential to be a time waster.

6. **Guilt.** Guilt is like anxiety—it almost always motivates you to do something of a lesser priority. You feel guilty so you go to the prayer meeting when you really have higher priority things to do with your family. Guilt makes you spend time with someone rather than rest or study. I've found that women are especially susceptible to guilt and it robs them of time that could be better invested.

Try not to let anyone (including your children) or anything manipulate you. Do what you do because it's a priority and not out of guilt. If your inner voice keeps saying, "You *should* have done that, you *should* do it over again, you *should* be more involved in the church, you *should* have prayed longer, you *should* have, you *should* have, you *should* have," just remind yourself that it's not the voice of your Father. The Spirit of God always *leads* you and doesn't condemn you. Don't give in to guilt but stay on course with the priorities that you have set.

7. **Television.** I'm shocked by statistics showing that the average household watches more than four hours of television every day. That's too much, even if they're watching Christian television stations or reruns of older, more wholesome programs. Your time inventory will show you, as it did me, how much actual time you spend watching television. What can you do if you cut your viewing in half? You can read more, learn a language, take a course, keep a daily journal, play games with your family, or go to bed earlier.

The Lord has helped me with the time I used to spend watching sports. I was a sports fanatic while I was growing up, never missing a game on television. But it has been years since I've watched an entire football game in one sitting. I still follow sports closely, but the time I invested in watching is being invested in other places. Truthfully, I haven't regretted it.

As we conclude this section, I urge you to conduct your time inventory. Study its results and take steps to better redeem your time. Identify your time wasters and work on reducing them. Then commit to keeping a daily to-do list in a time organization system of your choosing. Prioritize your lists, numbering them and checking each item off as you go. Adjust your outlook on life and time by meditating on the concepts of wisdom, stewardship, and dominion.

But don't get under condemnation if you fail, or if the struggle to turn things around is harder than you thought. You didn't learn these bad habits overnight, and they won't go away that quickly either as you seek to endeavor to discipline yourself.

I have emphasized the need for a *daily* to-do list, yet it's all too easy to lose control of one day, get very little done, and become discouraged. Yet the Lord Himself set a pattern for you to follow in Genesis when He completed His work in six days and rested on the seventh. If you keep in mind that the *day is the unit of work*, but the *week is the unit of accomplishment*, you won't be so discouraged over a bad day and will have incentive to focus on what you can get done in that particular week.

I was delighted to see Covey address this same concept:

You need a tool that encourages you, motivates you, actually helps you spend the time you need in Quadrant II [activities that are not urgent but important], so that you're dealing with prevention rather than prioritizing crises. In my opinion, the best way to do this is to organize your life on a weekly basis. You can still adapt and prioritize on a daily basis, but the fundamental thrust is organizing the week.

Organizing on a weekly basis provides much greater balance and context than daily planning. There seems to be implicit cultural recognition of the week as a single, complete unit of time. Business, education, and many other facets of society operate within the framework of the week, designating certain days for focused investment and others for relaxation or inspiration. The basic Judeo-Christian ethic honors the Sabbath, the one day out of every seven set aside for uplifting purposes.[11]

There were days when I accumulated a huge to-do list. Since I started thinking in terms of the week, however, I've spread things out over more days. In fact, as a pastor I took Thursdays off about 60% of the time. Looking at my week as a whole on Sunday night helped me to preserve my day off from "predators" and the lack of planning.

While this section has focused on time management, the next section will help you apply this discipline and skill so that you can be a more organized person in other areas of life as well.

SAMPLE TIME INVENTORY LOG

Begin Time	Activity - Category	Scheduled	Unscheduled	Interrupt?	Total Minutes
7:00	PRAYER & READING/SPIRITUAL	✓			60
8:00	MORNING PREP/PERSONAL	✓			30
8:30	STAFF MEETINGS	✓			30
9:00	CORRESPONDENCE	✓			40
9:40	TRIP HOME - FORGOT NOTES		✓	✓	20
10:00	TEXAS CONFERENCE PREP	✓			20
10:20	PHONE CALL			✓	3
10:23	TEXAS CONFERENCE PREP	✓			27
10:50	CRUISE WORK	✓			60
11:50	PHONE CALL/STAFF MTG.			✓	10
NOON	LUNCH/PERSONAL				60
1:00	MISC. PHONE CALLS			✓	10
1:10	CALIF. CONFERENCE PREP		✓		50
2:00	SOUTH AFRICA PLANNING	✓			15
2:15	CALIF. PHONE CALL			✓	22
2:37	CRUISE PHONE CALL			✓	20
3:00	PICK UP PROMO PICTURES		✓		40
3:40	CORRESPONDENCE			✓	20
4:00	PHONE APPOINTMENT	✓			50
4:50	PHONE CALLS			✓	10
5:00	DINNER	✓			45

1. Enter the approximate time you begin an activity.

2. Enter the name of the activity and its category—i.e. television/leisure, staff meeting/planning, telephone/interruption, etc.

3. check whether this was a scheduled or unscheduled activity and whether you consider it an interruption or not.

4. When you begin the next activity, enter the total number of minutes you spent on the previous activity.

5. At the end of the day or designated period of time, total the number of minutes over which you kept your log. Then add up the number of minutes in the various categories to get an overview of where your time actually is spent.

SAMPLE TIME INVENTORY LOG

Begin Time	Activity - Category	Scheduled	Unscheduled	Interrupt?	Total Minutes
5:45	T.V.		✓		45
6:30	CLASS READING	✓			60
7:30	SO. AMER. PHONE CALL			✓	35
8:05	PERSONAL FINANCES		✓		25
8:30	T.V.		✓		45
9:15	PHONE CALL/PERSONAL			✓	15
9:30	T.V.		✓		120
11:30	BED				

990 MINUTES TOTAL

- PRAYER/READING - 60 (6%) - INCREASE
- PERSONAL - 155 (15.7%) - O.K.
- PHONE - 140 (14%) - NEEDS TO BE REDUCED!
- CLASSWORK - 60 (6%) - O.K.
- PLANNING - 80 (8%) - OK
- STAFF - 40 (5%) - TOO LITTLE
- CONFERENCE WORK - 240 (24%) - GOOD!
- T.V. - 205 (21%) - TOO MUCH!
- CORRESPONDENCE - 60 (6%) - O.K.

1. Enter the approximate time you begin an activity.

2. Enter the name of the activity and its category—i.e. television/leisure, staff meeting/planning, telephone/interruption, etc.

3. check whether this was a scheduled or unscheduled activity and whether you consider it an interruption or not.

4. When you begin the next activity, enter the total number of minutes you spent on the previous activity.

5. At the end of the day or designated period of time, total the number of minutes over which you kept your log. Then add up the number of minutes in the various categories to get an overview of where your time actually is spent.

TIME INVENTORY LOG   DATE_____

Begin Time	Activity - Category	Scheduled	Unscheduled	Interrupt?	Total Minutes

1. Enter the approximate time you begin an activity.

2. Enter the name of the activity and its category—i.e. television/leisure, staff meeting/planning, telephone/interruption, etc.

3. check whether this was a scheduled or unscheduled activity and whether you consider it an interruption or not.

4. When you begin the next activity, enter the total number of minutes you spent on the previous activity.

5. At the end of the day or designated period of time, total the number of minutes over which you kept your log. Then add up the number of minutes in the various categories to get an overview of where your time actually is spent.

SECTION FOUR

ORGANIZATION: How To Stay On Top of Your "Lode"

"For acquiring a disciplined and prudent life"
—Proverbs 1:3

Chapter Seventeen

"I Can't Be Organized—I'm Creative!"

This chapter begins the section entitled "Organization: How To Stay On Top Of Your 'Lode.'" The word *lode* is a mining term that refers to a rich vein of ore. The first three sections of this book have urged you to mine your gold by finding your purpose, setting goals, and using your time for what matters most. That has hopefully increased your "lode"—the rich vein of opportunities and ideas that can make your life more meaningful and productive.

This fourth section will reinforce your need to improve your ability to stay on top of that lode before it weighs you down and simply adds to your frustration and anxiety. A renewed commitment to organize your world is critical if you are to follow through with what you've learned so far. But the skills and power to organize are just as important as the commitment itself. Many people aren't organized because they haven't been trained.

Like most people, you have probably been victimized at one time or another by someone who is disorganized—the mechanic who didn't do the repairs you requested, the catalog company that messed up your order, or your doctor's office that sent the incorrect paperwork to your insurance company. That disorganization may have cost you time and money and brought you great aggravation in the process.

Several recent instances of disorganization stand out in my mind, none earth-shaking but bothersome nonetheless. My wife and I use a check-writing system that has three checks on a page instead of the usual system with one. For eleven years, my bank has sent me the wrong checks whenever I've ordered more. No matter how I order or whom I talk to when I order, I invariably receive the wrong checks.

Another instance occurred after a church conference I helped organize. We left a number of boxes behind that needed to be returned to our office by UPS. When we departed, the church assured us that the boxes would be sent the following Monday. Numerous calls and six weeks later, someone finally got around to sending the boxes back.

Yes, even Christian organizations can be disorganized! When I lived in Orlando, I rented audio equipment on several occasions and always went to a Christian company to do so. When I walked in the door, I was invariably greeted by polite people who were quick to say, "Please" and "Thank you." But the place was a disorganized mess! The billing was almost always wrong, the paperwork was frequently lost, and the sales people never seemed to live up to their promises. My secretary and I always dreaded doing business there.

Contrast these cases with my experience on a recent trip to Australia, where our ministry team toured five cities in 14 days. The coordinator in Australia, Janet Parnwell, was wonderful to work with. Because we had so much musical equipment, each flight had to be closely coordinated not only for the passengers, but for the freight. Each meeting required the utmost communication with the local church staff. A lot could have gone wrong, but the entire tour was a real pleasure and came off without a hitch because Janet was painstakingly organized.

Organization, or the lack thereof, made the difference in each example mentioned above. In one case, Janet was able to stay on top of her lode. She minimized our stress and helped us minister effectively because of her attention to details. In the other cases, the people could not handle what they had and cost their organizations money, to say nothing of the inconvenience they caused me and others.

Or perhaps you have been victimized by another kind of disorganization—your own. Have you run out of excuses for lost reports, forgotten appointments, or missed opportunities? Are you tired of having to clean up the results of your own disorganization? If so, then this is the day that you can bring change to your life. This is the day that you can start down the road that leads to peace and joy through organization and self-discipline.

Let's define what I mean by organization. For this section, I will not refer to Covey's *The 7 Habits* since that book doesn't address the issue of organization. Instead I will enlist the help of Stephanie Winston and her book *The Organized Executive*. In that book, Winston lists some of the more commonly held **misconceptions about organization**:

- Order is a question of neat desks, straight rows of razor-sharp pencils, and precisely aligned stacks of paper.

- Orderliness is next to godliness. Disorganization indicates weakness and lack of moral fiber.

- To be sloppy and disorganized is to be creative.

- Disorganization is destiny.

- Organization requires an inflexible regimen.

- Organization is bureaucratic, related to nit-picking, and unworthy of people who are capable of thinking more grandly.[1]

I've had people tell me I'm organized because I was born that way. Many of the same people have told me that they were creative and couldn't be (or weren't interested in being) organized. (I could have taken that to mean that I wasn't creative because I was organized.) Some of those same people actually feared that organization would stifle or harm their creativity (thus the title for this chapter!).

It's true that I do have a propensity to organize and plan that was nurtured by disciplined and organized parents. But my sister was raised by the same parents, isn't nearly as "organized," yet worked efficiently and effectively for 33 years before her early retirement (at a young age, I might add, or I'll be in trouble with her). The nature of my work and the prompting of the Holy Spirit have caused me to design and develop my own organizational skills. The difference between my sister and me, raised by the same organized parents, helps clarify what organization is and isn't. Again I cite Stephanie Winston:

- Neatness and organization do not necessarily go together—it is a matter of style.

- Disorganization is neither in your fate nor in your genes. The ability to make sense of random data is a fundamental human attribute.

- Whether you are a good or bad person is not in question, and therefore guilt over disorganization is not appropriate. The propensity to disorder often reflects leftover traces of childhood rebellion to parental authority.

- Organization liberates, it does not constrict.

- Personal organization is a key trait of many successful people.

- Organizing *is, quite simply, a learned skill—a set of methods and tools with which to arrange your time and workload to meet your goals* (emphasis added).[2]

I agree with what Winston has written, yet I have one question that remains: If organization is a "learned skill," why don't more people learn it? On a more personal note, why aren't you more organized? Those questions can have many answers, but there is one solution: Organization is a spiritual discipline and has its roots in spiritual principles. Let's turn now to see what the Bible has to say about organization, develop our own biblical definition, and then address what needs to take place for you to become a more organized person.

Chapter Eighteen

Who Cares?

Kevin (not his real name) was an accident waiting to happen. Wearing a shirt pocket bulging with a small calendar and several pens, he gave the appearance that he was ready for anything. Yet over time, I came to refer to Kevin's calendar as the "black hole," for things he put in it somehow fell into oblivion and were never seen or heard from again.

Kevin was usually late and lost many things entrusted to his care. His office was filled with papers, books, and reports haphazardly stacked on any available open space. He meant well and was a likable fellow, so most people dismissed his disorder with a shake of their head and the phrase, "That's Kevin!"

Is organization a gift only distributed to a chosen few? Is it fair to expect Kevin and those like him to change? Is it just nit-picking to even expect Kevin to be organized? Does God really care how organized you are or aren't? Hopefully we can find answers to these questions as we study God's Word.

Let's begin with Paul's letter to the Corinthians, where he wrote, "For God is not a God of disorder but of peace" (1 Corinthians 14:33). Paul wrote those words while teaching the church how to conduct orderly public meetings. Yet it's a principle that can be applied beyond church services and indicates that God does indeed care about order and organization.

Gold Nugget Fifteen

"Locusts have no king, yet they advance together in ranks." —Proverbs 30:27

Genesis 1 reflects God's love for peace and order in creation. Disorganization and confusion are results of the fall of man and were not programmed through God's design. God is a God of order, and creation bears that out. The Lord established laws of physics that remain remarkably constant. Nature's food chain is an intricate, well-organized system that feeds countless numbers of organisms daily. The sun sets and rises according to schedule, and the seasons come and go. Some of life's greatest traumas come when God's order is challenged through a storm, earthquake, or other unexpected interruption. God is a God of order, and His order and organization bring peace.

But does God expect *you* to be organized? This can be answered when we read what Paul wrote to Timothy, "For God did not give us a spirit of timidity, but a spirit of *power*, of *love*, and of *self-discipline*" (2 Timothy 1:7, emphasis added). The Holy Spirit brings power to your life, power capable of changing you into a more organized person. The Spirit also brings *love*, and love focuses on the other person's well-being. This kind of love doesn't make someone else wait for an hour because you're habitually late. This love also doesn't forget birthdays, anniversaries, and other special occasions. Nor does it lose or ignore the reports and memos prepared by others.

Gold Nugget Sixteen

"For attaining wisdom and discipline; for understanding words of insight; for acquiring a disciplined and prudent life, doing what is right and just and fair." —Proverbs 1:2-3

In addition, the Spirit brings *self-discipline*. While most other translations use "sound mind," the NIV Bible uses the term "self-discipline," which represents a valid translation. Organizing your kitchen, garage, calendar, desk, or life is a matter of self-discipline, something at which the Spirit is an expert! If you need more discipline, the Spirit doesn't expect you to work it up on your own. He's there to help because self-discipline is part of His very nature. He wants to make it part of yours.

But just how important is organization in the scheme of life? To answer that, let's consider another verse, this one from the book of Psalms: "To him who orders his conduct aright, I will show the salvation of God" (Psalm 50:23, NKJV). The verb "orders" has the concept of organization at its root. If you put your world in order by doing what you can do, then God will "show you His salvation" by doing what He can do.

I need to organize because I need to see all of God's salvation I can on a daily basis. When I organize a conference, I work hard trying to go over every detail. Yet there are things that I forget to check or that "slip through the cracks" and have the potential to go wrong. Time and time again, I have seen the Lord intervene on my behalf. He has made me look good when I didn't deserve to look good. Why?

I believe it's because I tried to "order my way." I did all I could humanly do, and the Lord intervened to do the rest. My organization allows me to pray, "Lord, I've done all I can. I need your help." I'm not asking Him to get me out of a fix of my own making (although He has done that); I'm asking Him to help me in my weakness to get the job done. He hasn't failed me yet. He has shown me His "salvation" over and over again.

Just how important is organization in God's plan? Jesus ended His parable of the talents with the phrase, "Well done, good and *faithful* servant; you were *faithful* over a few things. Enter into the joy of your lord" (Matthew 25:21, NKJV emphasis added). I don't think order and organization are the most important principles in your walk with the Lord. Yet there's an aspect of organization that involves faithfulness, pure and simple. If you're faithful to be punctual (even early), you won't be racing around, then offering any number of excuses to those left waiting. You'll have peace and joy, knowing that you're being faithful, something the Lord requires and in which He delights.

I want to know the joy of my Lord by being faithful with what He has given me. From my calendar to my car, from my lunch appointments to my pulpit ministry, I want to be self-disciplined because it pleases Him and allows a flow of grace and blessing to come into my life. Furthermore, I don't want to be selfish and hurt others by forgetting or losing what's important to them.

So for our purposes, let's define organization as *ordering or removing all possible clutter, whether physical, mental, or spiritual, so that you can give your attention to your highest priority at the moment.*

The results of disorganization are spelled out in Proverbs 24:30-34:

> *I went past the field of the sluggard, past the vineyard of the man who lacks judgment; thorns had come up everywhere, the ground was covered with weeds, and the stone wall was in ruins. I applied my heart to what I observed and learned a lesson from what I saw: A little sleep, a little slumber, a little folding of the hands to rest—and poverty will come on you like a bandit and scarcity like an armed man.*

I'm convinced that many people experience lack or even suffer depression because they don't have the self-discipline to organize their world and the opportunities they have before them. Since *how* they handle these opportunities is the basis for receiving more, they cut themselves off from promotions and God's choicest blessings. They haven't been spiritually faithful with what they have, so God can't give them more.

Is your "field" overrun with weeds? Have you suffered financial loss due to your inability to manage what you have? In the next chapter we will look at one biblical concept to help you better understand why organization is important, and then we'll look at a plan of action that will allow you to enjoy all that God has for you.

Chapter Nineteen

First Comes the Natural

In Section Three, I described some of my experiences serving my pastor as part of my ministry training. I remember one particular season during that period of my life when I was depressed over my state of affairs. My depression came to a boil when I heard a message preached by Ern Baxter, who still stands as one of the finest preachers I've ever heard.

This particular message was about discipling the nations of the earth, one of Ern's favorite themes. Joseph, the man I was serving, had just returned from South Africa, and I had stayed home to care for things on the home front. Still disappointed that I didn't get to go to Africa, a heavy dose of self-pity set in after I heard that message and I began to complain to the Lord. I felt like ministry opportunities were passing me by as I stayed home "licking postage stamps and pulling weeds" (those were the exact words I used as I cried out from disappointment and disillusionment).

After Ern spoke that Sunday morning, I went to the prayer room for ministry but didn't receive any real comfort or help. When I got home, however, the Lord began to show me from His Word why He was training me the way He was. I found an appropriate verse in 1 Corinthians 15:46, "The spiritual did not come first, but the natural, and after that the spiritual."

As I have shared already, I was anxious, even ambitious, for spiritual responsibility and duties. That ambition wasn't wrong in itself, for Paul wrote to Timothy, "*If anyone sets his heart* on being an overseer, *he desires a noble task*" (1 Timothy 3:1, emphasis added). Paul didn't criticize the ambition for leadership; he simply outlined the price to be paid if that ambition was to be realized.

Part of my price to pay was organizing and being faithful over the responsibilities He gave me at home and with my pastor. If I would be faithful to care for the daily administration of duties at home and in the office, I would some day come into what I believed the Lord had for me. Before I would receive spiritual things, I had to be faithful with natural things.

Gold Nugget Seventeen

"A faithful man will be richly blessed, but one eager to get rich will not go unpunished." — Proverbs 28:20

From those years, I've come to realize that the Lord is ever faithful. He never gives you more than you can handle and He is always there to help you do what He assigns. Whenever I sign a Bible, book, or program for someone, I always add Hebrews 11:6 after my signature. I've already referred to that verse several times and it tells us that God rewards those who diligently seek Him.

If you're serious about self-discipline and organization and will seek the Lord for power and knowledge, then He is faithful and will reward you with what you need, just as He has me. Since those early days, I've come to grips with four tools and practices that have helped me be better organized, thus allowing me to increase my responsibilities and productivity. They have become weapons in my personal battle to bring order into my world.

1. A Time Management System

I've already discussed the need for a system to efficiently manage your time in the previous section. For me, however, my Franklin Covey system is more than a time management system. It's my focal point as I work to stay on top of my own lode.

As a young(er) man, I carried a planner in my back pocket for several years but didn't use it much. I would enter things to do (mostly things I was afraid I'd forget) and then forget to look at it for days at a time. Then I attended a Charles Hobbs' seminar in 1984 that taught me how to use the system more effectively. Something spiritual happened to me during the two days of that seminar.

There I was confronted with how scattered my world was. I saw that I couldn't possibly do any more than I was doing without some help. Charles Hobbs taught me how to use my time management system for more than time management. From that point on, I became more organized and efficient because I decided to go beyond what my memory could handle to a system that freed my mind for more creative things.

Today my Franklin Covey planner is seldom far from me. It contains a:

- two-page-per-month calendar for the current and next year
- two-page-per-day planner for the current and following month
- stamps, postcards, frequent flyer coupons, business cards, family pictures, blank paper, calculator, and ruler
- complete address and phone directory of all the people who are part of my world
- typed prayer list with names and issues of importance to my prayer life
- notebook dividers that contain and organize pulpit messages, notes and humorous stories needed for preaching, ministry budgets, long-range goals, school work, research projects, and family matters
- six-year planner complete with holidays and special occasions
- holder for receipts, letters to answer, and other current projects that require my attention

All this weighs under four pounds and is easy to carry and keep track of. With this in hand, I don't have to expend much energy trying to find something. It's right at my fingertips whenever I need to refer or add to it. My calendar is filled in with birthdays, anniversaries, and other important occasions. I lost my planner once, but I had most of its contents copied and stored in a safe. Today I am learning to use a Palm Pilot™.

I can honestly say that the Lord has helped me learn how to use my planner. Until 1984, I carried it as a formality. Since then I have carried it out of necessity, not in bondage to it, but in recognition of its helpfulness and usefulness. And my philosophy since then has been to solidify as much of my world into that notebook as possible. By doing that, I have been able to face my responsibilities with joy and confidence.

2. Computer

While I was a senior in college, I took a computer programming course and almost flunked. I had never received less than a "B" grade in four years, but the computer language FORTRAN almost extended my college career.

When the personal computer first came on the scene, I viewed it with fear (based on my college experience) and as an intrusion into modern man's life. I saw friends become consumed with their new computers and their operation. I heard horror stories of hard drives "crashing," taking with them countless hours of irretrievable work. On top of all that, I looked at the price tag and decided that the computer wasn't for me.

Then I went through a major job transition in 1988 that cost me my secretary. Without Shelley to keep track of my notes, letters, and memos, I was faced with a serious problem. I now had to begin doing my own work, and using a typewriter was out of the question.

During this transition, my employer agreed to buy me a computer; before I knew it, I had an IBM "clone" with a dot matrix printer, WordPerfect software, and a set of manuals. Shelley gave me a crash course, and I was on my own.

Gold Nugget Eighteen

"Where there are no oxen, the manger is empty, but from the strength of an ox comes an abundant harvest." —Proverbs 14:4

Those early days were frustrating since I lost documents due to ignorance and carelessness. At times, it took me hours to print a one-page letter, but I refused to give up. As I read, asked, experimented, and listened, I gradually began to get the hang of it.

In a few months, I was cranking out a lot of work. Then I began experimenting with other software besides word processing. I started storing and accessing names and addresses for meetings I organized in special meeting planner data files. Next I tackled a time management system and began to prioritize to-do lists for special events and conferences.

After several years, the Lord blessed me with a portable computer, a 17-pound model that went with me everywhere I went, including Latin America and the Caribbean. While a bit cumbersome, that computer allowed me to take my office on the road. I could now continue my work away from home and start projects that could be completed when I returned.

Today I use a laptop computer that weighs only a few pounds. I've learned, through a series of videos, how to use a spreadsheet program that has enabled me to do more budget and financial work. In addition, I have a portable printer that enables me to print out letters, schedules, and memos on the road. With those tools, I earned my doctorate, completing all my outlines, book reports, and papers. As an added bonus, I've written four books (including this one) and kept up with most of my correspondence while on the road.

My point in sharing this history with you is this: If I can learn to use these items, so can you. You must master any fear you have of technology if you are going to organize your life in today's world. I can't imagine how I could do what I do if I didn't have a computer. Now don't ask me how it works and don't expect any detailed explanations from me of its intricacies. But I've learned what I've needed to learn, and it has revolutionized my world.

Let me add that you must also overcome the cost factor as you consider how you can make a computer part of your life. While the costs have come down, computer equipment and other technological aids still aren't inexpensive. I've had to pray for my computers and even purchase some of them by making payments. But in the long run, my computer, printer, and software have increased my productivity and income. And the Lord has been faithful to provide for me in miraculous ways. We'll discuss that in more detail in the next section on faith.

3. "When in Doubt...Throw It Out"

My family and I relocated three times between 1989 and 1993. Moving is always a traumatic experience full of the unknown as you pack all your belongings, watch strangers carry them to a truck, watch them carry them into another house, and then unpack them all. You have to be careful not to throw anything away as you discard the packing and boxes and must also watch for damage.

But moving that often forced me to make a decision about what needed to make the transition and what didn't. Prior to packing for each move, I went through all my files and threw away a lot of papers, publications, and reports. I also went through my books each time and gave away some to charity, friends, and colleagues.

My guideline was this: If I hadn't referred to it, read it, or used it in the last 12 months, then chances are I wouldn't need it ever again. I also asked myself where I could get the item in question if I ever did need it again. If I hadn't looked at it in a year, or if I could locate it somewhere else with reasonable ease, I threw it out.

(I've also followed the same procedure with my computer. I regularly go through all my files and delete letters, memos, reports, and budgets more than a year old that were just sitting on my hard disk. In most cases, I didn't even save them on a floppy disk to store somewhere else; I discarded them.)

My wife and children also followed the same procedure. Several times we had yard sales, selling household and personal items that we no longer needed. All in all, our moves were streamlined because we did away with "stuff" that has a tendency to accumulate over time.

I include this principle in this chapter because it has helped me to organize my world by giving me less to organize. And I've found that I can get attached to things just because they belong to me, even though they have no real use or value.

Here's what I mean. One Christmas as I was praying and bemoaning the fact that I didn't have gifts for my leadership team and friends, I felt the Holy Spirit impress me with the thought, "You have a lot of nice books." I thought it strange and agreed that I did indeed have a nice library. I continued praying about my Christmas dilemma, however, only to have this thought come back again and again.

Then it dawned on me. The Lord was showing me that I did have plenty of Christmas presents if only I would part with some of my books. My initial response was that I may need those books one day. But in obedience, I went through my library, pulled out a number of my bigger hardbacks, wrapped them, and gave them away. They were a blessing to others, and I've never needed one of those books since.

On another occasion, I was telling the Lord that I would like to give a special offering to a ministry that was near and dear to my family and me. Knowing that my funds were low, I was asking the Lord to provide something I could give. As I prayed, I was reminded of my silver dollar collection that I had had since I was a boy. Surely the Lord wasn't implying that I should give away my silver dollars!

The Lord wasn't implying anything, but I began to see that I was attached to those coins. They were important to me, yet my Father owns all the silver and gold. I talked with my wife, prayed some more, and then sold those coins for $400. I had my offering.

Jesus stated that your heart will be where your treasure is. I don't want my heart tied up in a lot of things and possessions. Remember that organization is the removal of all clutter, whether physical or spiritual, so that you can give your attention to your highest priority. Personally, I want to be preoccupied with the kingdom of God. Getting rid of as much as possible whenever possible has been a good spiritual practice and a valuable organizational one as well. Three moves in five years helped solidify that principle in my heart.

Why save old magazines? How many years of clippings, budgets, and messages on cassette tape must you have to really carry out your purpose and goals? I'm not suggesting that you follow my one-year rule, but you should develop your own philosophy that will guide you in your decision to keep or discard.

4. Delegation

There's an old saying that goes, "If you want something done right, do it yourself." I find that's the motto of many people to whom I teach time management and organization. They feel that there is much that only they can do or keep track of, and thus they feel their schedules and lives are "maxed out."

There was a time when I felt the same way. I ran myself ragged trying to do all things and be all things to the people who mattered to me. This led to some periods of pretty intense burnout, when my mind would actually stop functioning with any kind of effectiveness. I would be irritable, forgetful, and spend a lot of energy doing just a few things.

Then I began to study the principle of delegation as it was presented in Acts 6, the passage we looked at in our discussion of effectiveness in Section One. If you remember, the Grecian widows were being neglected in the daily distribution of food, and the church came to the apostles to find a solution to that problem.

The apostles, however, didn't get involved in the problem directly. They delegated the responsibility to seven deacons to serve the church as effective ministers and servants to the widows. The apostles could not neglect their purpose in the Word and prayer to "wait on tables," and the result was that the church grew and the Word spread.

Perhaps you're caught in the "I'm-the-only-one-who-can-get-it-done-right" syndrome. Or perhaps you have a time management system, a computer, and are disciplined to organize your life, and can't possibly see how you could handle any more than you're doing right now. The answer may lie in delegating some of your current duties and responsibilities to someone else.

I remember when my wife, Kathy, returned to graduate school and was very busy with schoolwork. She is also a conscientious housewife and spent many hours providing a wonderful home environment for me and our two children. And she suffers a bit from the "do-it-yourself" mind-set. But something had to give, so she had to institute some changes.

Kathy trained our 15 year old daughter to cook, and Deborah had regular kitchen duty. When Kathy realized how much time she was spending washing and ironing, she decided to trust the Lord for the money to have my shirts professionally laundered. She also learned to utilize our 17 year old son (who had recently learned to drive) to run errands and help with his sister's transportation needs.

You may not delegate because no one can do that job as well as you can. In a nutshell, that's either pride or true. You don't know for a fact whether someone else can learn to do it like you until you release it to their care. And if that task isn't done the way you would prefer, how important is the way it was done as long as the end result is acceptable? Pride will cause you to think that no one can do it like you can.

If it's true that no one else can do the job like you can, then you may need to invest some time in the short term to train someone and still carry out the task. You can be sure that there will be times when the person to whom you've delegated messes up, causing you to have to re-do the project.

Properly releasing those tasks, however, frees you in the long run to do other things and concentrate on more important tasks. That in itself is worth the price of working a little harder now to train someone new.

The greatest example of delegation in the Bible is provided by Jesus Himself. After three and one-half years of training His disciples, Jesus returned to the Father. At a time when his treasurer killed himself, and all the apostles ran and cowered in fear, his vice president denied he ever knew Jesus. But Jesus delegated the responsibility for the church to that group of men and went on to glory! How could He do this and leave at such a critical hour?

He did it because He understood that the Holy Spirit was a *Paraclete*, one called alongside to help. In faith, Jesus entrusted certain tasks to His followers because He knew they would not be alone. The people to whom you delegate won't be alone either if you delegate properly. Train them, be there to help them, pray for them, and then support them by lovingly distancing yourself so that they can learn the way you did—from experience. If you can do that, you will find your ability to organize will increase because you don't have to have a hands-on role in every task, whether at home, in the church, or in the office.

I appreciate the importance of delegation even more after my recent transition. Two years before I knew I would leave, I brought another man on staff at the church. Fred had been with me since my early ministry days, but found himself languishing in the grocery business. It was important to me to begin training my successor, even though I had no immediate plans to leave. So although it didn't make financial sense to add another mouth to feed, I brought Fred on staff. I did my best from then on to train Fred for the day when he would be the senior pastor.

We traveled together to prisons and discussed ministry philosophies and techniques. I encouraged Fred to pursue his degree and agreed to help financially. In the office, I went over the finances and gave him my approach to building and keeping the budget.

While I was still in Florida, Fred played an important role by filling in during my times away. And when the call came for me to relocate to another city, I already had someone with my vision and heart to take over and continue the work.

Even though I delegated that church to Fred, I stayed in close contact. I offered advice and encouragement when needed (and asked for). I helped provide continuity during the transition and returned to preach several times a year. Delegation isn't abandoning the situation or the person to whom you've delegated the job.

I enlisted my time management system as an aid during this process. I maintained a page with Fred's name on it and that helped me keep track of things we discussed, and things he was working on. I also wrote his name on my to-do list to call regularly. Delegation does free you to do more because more people are doing the work. It doesn't always release you from oversight of those delegated tasks.

These four things—a time management system, a computer, throwing things away, and delegation—have been my major weapons in the war against disorder. I share them with the hope that they will help you as they have me. In the next chapter, I will share some other organizational ideas that will hopefully help you as well. Before we go there, however, I want to pray that the Paraclete will come beside you now to help you as you seek to order your world.

Lord, I ask that you would send the Holy Spirit into the life of each reader. Let the Spirit be the Paraclete and come alongside to help each person. Grant each one more self discipline to be able to organize their calendar, home, work areas, and desks. Show each person how to work smarter and better. Help them identify a time management system and how to use or better use a computer. Reduce the hold that things may have on them and then help them delegate where it's appropriate. And give them a desire to continue to improve their skills as they organize their lives. Amen.

Chapter Twenty

A Treasure Chest of Ideas

Organization is a personal matter, and I offer the following ideas for two reasons. First, I hope that you will take one or two and apply them to your life where they fit. Second, I want to stimulate your thinking to develop your own helpful and creative guidelines.

One basic rule that's critical to organization is to assign everything a place, and to work diligently to return those things to their proper place. This means that you must purchase drawer dividers or containers, closet organizers, and hanging file folders. Then label each container. When the container becomes full, it's time to sort it out, keep what is still needed, and toss or box the rest for storage. With that in mind, let's dig into this treasure chest of organizational ideas.

1. In the Home

1. As mentioned in the previous section, use your time management system for home matters as well as office and ministry. Make a prioritized list of things to do even for weekends when you are home. Write down simple tasks that you can easily forget, such as changing the furnace air filter. Keep *one* calendar with all important appointments (doctors, dentists, school, business), birthdays, anniversaries, and other events.

2. Try to do two things at once whenever possible. For instance, while you work around the home, listen to cassettes and work toward learning a new language. While watching television, catch

up on your casual reading, muting the sound during commercials and other breaks.

3. See if there is any job you can do around the house that will earn money while you do your regular housework such as baby-sitting, sewing, laundry and ironing, or pet sitting. This will make doing two things at once profitable for you and allow you to have some money to invest in another degree, a computer, or other things that will help you be more productive.

4. Get young children to bed early. This will give you more time to do what you need or like to do.

5. Review your calendar regularly with your spouse, children, or roommate. Longer drives in the car are good times to do this.

6. Experiment to see if you can function on one-half hour less sleep than you get now.

7. Cut in half the time you invest watching television.

8. Develop regular habits for where to place your mail, bills, glasses, car keys, and household tools. This will save you the time it takes to look for those things that can be easily misplaced.

9. Choose a set day and time to pay your household bills, do the laundry and ironing, have family time, and conduct personal study. Our family time was Saturday night (before the teenage years arrived), and I still pay bills and write checks every Sunday evening.

10. Lock your car only with your keys. If you've ever locked your keys in your car, you'll understand what I mean. Keep a spare key in a specially designed magnetic box somewhere on the outside of the car (where it won't be found by thieves).

11. Involve your children in the process of organizing. Have them clean out their rooms regularly, pick up after themselves, and set certain days for special chores. Help them organize their school work and assignments.

12. For older children, help them work through the process of setting priorities. Have them list all the things they must do, and then help them choose which is most important. Don't decide for them, and let them make mistakes so they will learn how to manage their time efficiently.

13. Take reading with you wherever you go just in case you are delayed unexpectedly. This will allow you to use time that would otherwise be wasted.

14. Plan your weekends one week in advance and vacations at least six months in advance.

15. Put an "X" through certain days on your calendar for personal or family time, or for a day of rest. When someone approaches you to do something, you can honestly say you have something else planned.

16. As the school year begins, merge the school calendar with your own and try to keep those days when the children are off free from distractions.

17. Let your children have a day every once in a while that they can plan and do what will bless them.

18. When you travel, take at least one day's work with you in case you get delayed due to weather, equipment problems, or other circumstances beyond your control.

19. Purchase an "accordion file" and label each pocket with a category for your receipts. My file has the following categories: auto, housing, professional, medical, medicines, interest paid, income, and other records. All during the year, my wife and I place our receipts we will need for tax purposes in the appropriate pocket. At tax time, it takes only a few hours to pull all our information together. You can use envelopes or files to do the same thing.

20. Work out a system for paying your bills. My mail is placed on my desk at home when it arrives. I open it, throw out the inserts

and outer envelope, and then place all bills to pay in one drawer. Every Sunday night I sit down and sort through the bills that need to be paid that week. When I go out of town, I write the checks, seal the envelopes, and then write the date for Kathy to mail it on the back flap.

2. In the Office

1. Begin each work day by organizing your day—before you pick up the phone, read the paper, or even turn on your computer. If you put off this task, the day will slip away from you. Fifteen minutes invested at 8 a.m. will pay off many times over by 5 p.m.

2. Make a commitment to maintain an organized and clutter-free desk or work area. Take one day to set your work area in order and sort through your files and closets. MacKenzie writes, "Get rid of the notion that a loaded desk is the sign of a very busy, very important person. It's a sign of nothing but disorganization."[3]

3. Try to touch your paperwork and mail as few times as possible so as not to let piles of "stuff" accumulate. Try writing answers to letters and memos by writing on the original copy you receive. This won't work in all cases, of course, but when it does, it will save you having to type a separate response.

4. Maintain a simple but adequate filing system. Be ruthless with what you discard, and also have a "to do," "to read," and "to file" file. Place paperwork in these files and then attend to them once a week (remember to do this by making it an action item on one day's to-do list). Your "to read" file is perfect to take on planes or other visits when you know you'll have some time to spare.

5. Keep files that you touch regularly in your desk file drawer. Place less used files in a file cabinet close to your desk. Store seldom-used files in a place that's out of sight or some distance from your work area. Use as many files as you need to give everything that's important to you a place of its own.

6. Set a time limit and have a precise agenda for each meeting you call. If you aren't in charge of the meeting, you can still have your

own agenda that you submit to your supervisor prior to the meeting or that you wish to address in the meeting.

7. Sit down immediately after a meeting and make a list of all that you must do as a result of that meeting. If something isn't clear, resolve it immediately before no one remembers exactly what was decided.

8. Reward yourself with a pleasant task or a break after you have completed an unpleasant one.

9. Constantly improve your computer skills and upgrade your hardware and software to take advantage of new technology.

10. Don't forget to clean your hard disk of unneeded files and letters every now and then, so that your computer speed will be all that it should be.

11. Get into the habit of backing up your computer files at least once a week, or more frequently if your work demands it. (Write "back up" on a future to-do list so you won't have to rely on your memory as to when you need to back up again). If appropriate, back up your day's work as the last thing you do for the day.

12. Get rid of your desk blotter. The temptation to write things down on it is too great, and the things you write there can be easily discarded or not with you when away from your desk. Likewise, don't use "yellow sticky notes" in place of your calendar or organizing system. That's not what they're intended for.

13. Keep a copy of important papers in a fireproof safe or at least in another location from where they're normally kept. That includes the computer disks onto which you have backed up your files.

14. Consider employing a time management or organizational consultant to come to your office and evaluate and recommend improvements for your company's organizational skills and habits. Once this is done, consider annual brush-up training.

3. Another Look at Household Organization From an Organized Woman—My Wife, Kathy!

My wife is organized, but doesn't follow the same system or rules that I do. With that in mind, I asked her to share some things that have made a difference for her as she has organized her world.

1. Plan meal menus one week in advance and do your grocery shopping accordingly. This saves time and repeated trips to the store.

2. Carry your coupons with you but don't become a slave to them. Don't travel 20 minutes to save a dime. Your time is worth something, too!

3. Stock up on staples and, as your budget allows, restock before you run out. Have the basics on hand to whip up a meatless meal, cake, or batch of cookies in a hurry.

4. Have a supply of food and other items in case of an emergency.

5. Keep a list near you at all times. Discipline yourself to jot down items when you think of them.

6. Prepare ahead of time for overnight guests. Make and freeze coffee cakes, desserts, deboned chicken breasts, sauces, casseroles, and extra ice before they come. Build up a supply of "sample-size" toiletries for your guests' everyday needs.

7. To save time on wash day, take freshly washed and dried linens and towels right out of the dryer and put them back onto the bed and towel rack. It saves the time of folding.

8. If you or your spouse travel regularly, keep a separate toiletry kit for your suitcase. Replenish it with half-used bottles and jars from your regular supply to cut down on weight. Also pack each shirt, suit, pair of pants, and dress in its own plastic bag available from a dry cleaners. The clothes will stay wrinkle-free and not need ironing upon arrival.

9. If you must choose between keeping your home "picked up" or cleaning a particular room, choose keeping your home neat. Go to particular cleaning tasks as you are able at a later time.

10. Periodically go through kitchen cabinets, making sure utensils are in the most convenient spot for your work habits and kitchen design.

11. Learn to use a computer. Don't be discouraged when you make mistakes.

12. Keep working with your children so that they develop self-discipline around the home. Don't give up!

13. Read, reread, and study Proverbs 31. There was a busy, industrious and faithful woman!

4. Still More Organization From Sue McMillin

As I mentioned earlier, you may want to enlist the help of an organizational consultant. One such consultant is Sue McMillin, from Fairfax, Virginia. Sue founded and directs *With Time to Spare*, a consulting firm that both educates and offers practical assistance to corporations and individuals who need organizational assistance. I asked Sue for a short list of her favorite organizational tips, which are included here. Readers can contact Sue by writing *With Time to Spare*, 654 S. Broadway, Georgetown, KY or by calling (502) 863-4221. Her fax number is (502) 865-2113 and website is www.withtimetospare.com.

Your Time

1. Use a notebook to record your thoughts, ideas, things to do, and people to call.

2. Brainstorm with friends and associates. If you're having trouble organizing your schedule, find a friend who excels in that area of life and ask for his/her help.

3. Break large projects into bite-size pieces and schedule them ac-

cordingly. In that way seemingly insurmountable tasks become more manageable.

4. Finish each project (or a segment of it) before you begin another—finish the paragraph before starting another letter, finish the dishes before starting the mending, etc.

5. Make sure you have a Sabbath. One day of rest will revitalize and refresh you so you will be more effective the other six days.

Home and Office

1. Assign everything its own place. If you don't have a place for your possessions, you will not be able to put them away.

2. Use stackable trays to sort your current mail. Mark them "to do," "to call," "to pay," etc.

3. Make sure you and your children have a personal office or work area in your home where you can keep and work on personal papers and projects.

4. Use a shoe bag (one with pockets) to organize cleaning supplies, mittens, tools, crafts, etc.

5. Use a lazy susan in the refrigerator.

6. Use boxes to store all your "stuff" in the basement.

7. Use drawer dividers to sort all your belongings in drawers.

5. Recommended Reading

For more guidelines and ideas on how to organize your world:

1. *How to Get Organized When You Don't Have the Time* by Stephanie Culp.
2. *Manage Your Time, Your Work, Yourself* by Merrill and Donna Douglas.
3. *The Time Trap* by Alec MacKenzie.

4. *Getting Organized* by Stephanie Winston.
5. *The Organized Executive* by Stephanie Winston.

Gold Nugget Nineteen

"Go to the ant, you sluggard; consider its ways and be wise! It has no commander, no overseer or ruler, yet it stores its provisions in summer and gathers its food at harvest." —Proverbs 6:6-8

Use the ant as an example. Go for it and organize what you have and what you do to the glory of God!

Chapter Twenty-One

"But Jesus Said…"

When my youngest was small, she would go to her brother and tell him to do something. When he refused, she should tack on the phrase "Dad said" and he would reluctantly do what she wanted, not wanting to disobey what she had represented me as saying.

I feel that's where I am with you as we finish this section. If you're convinced that you need to be more organized, then you may want to skip this chapter and proceed to Section Five. If you're not convinced, I want to make one last appeal and tell you that "Jesus said" you must pay attention to organization. My hope is that those words will spur you to action. For me, my instruction on organization would be incomplete without Jesus' words found in Luke 16:

> Whoever can be trusted with very little can also be trusted with much, and whoever is dishonest with very little will also be dishonest with much. So if you have not been trustworthy in handling worldly wealth, who will trust you with true riches? And if you have not been trustworthy with someone else's property, who will give you property of your own? (Luke 16:10-12)

The first principle that Jesus outlined is that *how you handle the little things determines if you will receive more*. I have come to realize that punctuality, remembering special occasions, timeliness in submitting work and reports, care for vehicles, homes, and possessions, and faithfulness to carry out small tasks diligently and completely are all important and not secondary traits. They may seem like little things, but faithfulness where these are concerned gives a good indication of how I will handle greater things.

It's important to note that many people don't want more than what they have. Some pastors and members don't want a bigger church, some music directors don't want a larger choir, some business owners don't want a larger business, some students don't want any more degrees, and some leaders don't want more responsibility.

I'm not saying that's wrong in every situation if that person knows his/her limitations and doesn't want to exceed them to simply have more. But increase and promotion seem to be what the Lord has in mind for His people and to turn that down can be wrong if it's the will of God.

In Matthew 25:23, those in the parable who were faithful with their talents were told, "You have been faithful with a few things; I will put you in charge of many things." Those who were faithful with their talents were also told, "Because you have been trustworthy in a very small matter, take charge of ten cities" (Luke 19:17). Jesus told the disciples that they would sit on 12 thrones and judge the 12 tribes of Israel. In each case, the Lord's idea of a reward for faithfulness was to give more responsibility and possessions.

If your mentality doesn't have room for more, then maybe you need to adjust your mentality. If you study the word "increase" in the New Testament, you'll see it connected with grace, knowledge, and love. The book of Proverbs says, "A large population is a king's glory, but without subjects a prince is ruined" (14:28). Your royal position, as we discussed in Section Three, requires that you have something to rule; a lack of "subjects" leads to a prince's demise. Increase is to be a way of life for the followers of the King.

The next principle Jesus described in Luke 16 is **faithfulness in financial matters**. The powerful connection between finances and spiritual things has always intrigued me and caused me to strongly emphasize financial matters in my preaching and teaching. Jesus implied that the Father isn't about to entrust true spiritual riches to someone who can't handle money.

This doesn't mean that you must have a lot of money to be worthy of spiritual riches. It simply means you must be faithful with what you have.

When I pastored in Orlando, our church was going through a lean financial season. During this time, I attended a conference and ran into a pastor friend who asked me how things were going. When I told him how tight things were, without hesitation, he began to share how the tendency is to cut back on giving during lean times. I realized that's exactly what I had done! He went on to explain what a mistake that is and encouraged me to catch up on my giving so that the blessing of the Lord could be released.

As hard as that was to hear, I knew that he spoke the truth, and Luke 16:11 was the proof. I went home and made good on all our commitments, and ensured that all future commitments would be paid in a timely manner, whether I got paid or not. If I wanted true riches in the church—people, ministry, finances—I knew the church had to be faithful with worldly wealth in order to see them come to pass. I'm glad to report that the church in Orlando experienced an exciting revival shortly thereafter, and I attribute it to our continued giving even through the tough times.

I believe that because many times bills aren't paid and financial commitments aren't kept due to disorganization. Fundraising consultants will tell you that Christians pay about 70% of the money that they pledge to organizations and activities. I'm convinced that much of the unpaid portion is due to the lack of organization in churches and personal lives that would help make it possible for these commitments to be honored. If you can't be faithful with unrighteous mammon, who will give you true riches? God won't, that's for sure.

The third principle in Luke 16 is *being faithful with that which belongs to someone else*. If I understand Luke 16:12 correctly, my faithful handling of the affairs of others will be the pathway to receive my own. I must be organized so that I will handle properly what's important to my pastor, my boss, my wife, my children, and my friends.

As I began to serve my pastor Joseph in my early years, the Lord wanted me to treat his possessions, ministry itinerary, and finances as if they were my own. If I could do that, then the Word promised me my own. If I could not, then the Lord was not obligated to entrust me with any natural or spiritual responsibilities of my own.

All this gave me tremendous incentive to sharpen my organizational skills. I saw that the Lord was going to promote me not through preaching, seminary, or teaching at a Bible school. My path to more was adherence to the principles found in Luke 16:10-12: attention to details, faithful use of money, and responsible oversight of that which belonged to another.

I have further seen how these principles were present in King David's life, thus allowing the Lord to use and promote him from the flocks to the throne of Israel. David was a creative genius who had tremendous practical responsibilities. It would be good to use him as a model as we attempt to come to grips with the importance of organization as a means to promotion in the Lord.

Few lives are given the attention that David's life receives in the Bible. His life story is put forth in four different books: 1 and 2 Samuel, 1 Kings, and 1 Chronicles. In addition, we have the book of Psalms, to which David made significant contributions, and the books of Proverbs and Ecclesiastes, which exist in part through David's influence on his son Solomon. Jesus adds to our body of knowledge about King David as He referred to King David in His own public ministry.

We first see David as a young man being anointed by Samuel as the replacement for King Saul in 1 Samuel 16. We then follow his progress to the throne as he served as a shepherd, defeated Goliath, served in Saul's court and army, endured relentless persecution from Saul, fled for his life, became king of the tribe of Judah, and finally ascended to the throne of Israel that God had promised him.

Then we read how David established his kingdom, fell through his adulterous and murderous union with Bathsheba, fled the treachery of his son, Absalom, and finally turned the kingdom over to his son, Solomon, just prior to his death.

We see that David was not only a king, but also a songwriter, poet, politician, statesman, warrior, father, husband, and prophet. His preparation to perform all these roles with distinction, however, wasn't the finest university or Bible school. His father didn't serve in these positions and then impart to him a vast amount of experience and information. He had no books or cassettes to which he could refer.

The Lord prepared David by means of a thorough education in the principles found in Luke 16:10-12. David's success was in large part due to his faithfulness to organize his world, even when it was small and seemingly insignificant. With that in mind, David's experience may have some similarities to your own as the Lord prepares you for His work.

Let's start with the principle of *"faithful in little, faithful in much."* We first see David as the shepherd over his father Jesse's sheep in Bethlehem. I always romantically pictured David caring for thousands of sheep spread over many hillsides, being assisted by other shepherds as he managed his father's rather large estate.

Then I saw a verse that changed my whole picture of that time in David's life. David, at his father's request, went to visit his three older brothers as the armies of Israel squared off against Goliath and his armies. Eliab, David's oldest brother, was not exactly glad to see him and sharply rebuked him with these words: "Why have you come down here? And with whom did you leave *those few sheep in the desert?* I know how conceited you are and how wicked your heart is; you came down only to watch the battle" (1 Samuel 17:28, emphasis added).

David wasn't tending thousands of sheep; he had responsibility for only a handful! This king-in-training began his kingly studies by watching over a few measly sheep. And he had to do that in the desert! I can only imagine the heat and difficulty in finding pasture as he cared for his father's flock.

David's encounter with Goliath revealed his faithfulness in caring for this little flock. When he met with Saul shortly after his brother said those hurtful things, David had this to say when the king questioned David's ability to fight Goliath:

> Your servant has been keeping his father's sheep. When a lion or a bear came and carried off a sheep from the flock, I went after it, struck it and rescued the sheep from its mouth. When it turned on me, I seized it by its hair, struck it and killed it (1 Samuel 17:34-35).

David risked his life for those few sheep. If I were David, perhaps I would have been tempted to write off any loss as a business loss. After all, my reasoning would have been, there were bound to be some unavoidable deaths among the flock under those conditions. Why risk my life for a little lamb?

David wasn't of that mind, however, but understood Luke 16

before it was ever written. He was determined to be faithful over a little. Is that your attitude as well? Do you carry out even your smallest responsibilities with the same care and diligence as David did? Are you training your children that diligence in details is preparation for handling greater responsibilities?

I can remember the first Bible study group of four people that I led. I wanted more responsibility but applied this principle to their care. I worked on the lessons for those four people like I would have for ministry to a large church. God prepared me to pastor my own church by teaching me to care for those four people.

David went from having responsibility for those sheep to being leader over the 400 in Adullam's cave, to being king over one tribe, and finally to ruling all Israel. He was able to organize hundreds of thousands of troops and carry out the work of his kingdom, which extended well beyond the borders of Israel. David did this because he started on the right foot: He took small things seriously and because he did, God anointed him to handle more.

Consider also the principle of being *"faithful with unrighteous mammon."* When Solomon was ready to build the Temple, David brought out his checkbook:

> *My son Solomon, the one whom God has chosen, is young and inexperienced. The task is great, because this palatial structure is not for man but for the Lord God. With all my resources I have provided for the temple of my God—gold for the gold work, silver for the silver, bronze for the bronze, iron for the iron and wood for the wood, as well as onyx for the settings, turquoise, stones of various colors, and all kinds of fine stone and marble—* all of these in large quantities. *Besides, in my devotion to the temple of my God I now give my personal treasures of gold and silver for the temple of my God, over and above everything I have provided for this holy temple: three thousand talents of gold (gold of Ophir) and seven thousand talents of refined silver, for the overlaying of the walls of the buildings, for the gold work and the silver work, and for all the work to be done by the craftsmen. Now, who is willing to consecrate himself today to the Lord?* (1 Chronicles 29:1-5, emphasis added).

At today's gold and silver prices, David gave a billion-dollar offering from his own bank account. Having done that, he challenged others to do the same.

How did David get such wealth? God, of course, chose to give it to him. It wasn't only through shrewd investments or his many foreign conquests; it was through his faithful oversight of what little he had in the early days.

I saw this truth when I was studying the story of David and Abigail. Abigail eventually became David's wife, but when the Bible first introduces her, she was married to Nabal, whose name means "worthless fool." In 1 Samuel 25, David's servants came to ask Nabal for some provisions for the troops. Nabal foolishly and arrogantly refused and sent them away empty-handed.

One of Nabal's servants reported to Abigail what Nabal had done, saying, "Yet these men were very good to us. They did not mistreat us, and the whole time we were out in the fields near them *nothing was missing*" (1 Samuel 25:15, emphasis added). David's men were actually protecting Nabal's flocks and servants just by being in the area, yet David did not feel free to take anything that belonged to Nabal. He could have "borrowed" a lamb for a midnight snack, taking payment for protective services rendered.

David and his men were faithful with Nabal's wealth, and because they were, God gave them true riches. David became a wealthy man because he was faithful to protect the riches of someone else.

Are you faithful with another man's money, as well as your own? Are you prompt to pay the bank its money when it's due? Do you protect your employer's interests by not wasting supplies, opportunities, or time? If you want true riches that are yours, then you must properly care for worldly wealth.

The final principle is *"faithful with another's and you will get your own."* It's well documented that David cared for Saul's kingdom as if it were his own, even after that kingdom had been promised to him! After Saul tried to kill him, David faithfully continued to dispatch his duties as court musician. While Saul used his army to pursue David, David used his army to defend and liberate the city of Keilah (see 1 Samuel 23). Saul should have been doing the liberating instead of trying to kill his successor!

These principles—faithful in little, faithful in finances, and faithful with what belongs to someone else—are essential if you are to understand why you need to "stay on top of your lode." God is using your paperwork, deadlines, church volunteer activities, and small tasks to train you for what is yet ahead. Organize your desk, garage, kitchen, and dorm room, and keep your possessions in good working order. Keep careful track of your calendar and appointments. Don't despise these small things, but carry them out to the best of your abilities.

There remains one final aspect to comprehend if you want to mine the real gold in your life. Your purpose, goals, time, and organization can be understood only in the context of faith, without which no one can please the Lord. Let's close this section now and turn our attention to a study of faith as the fifth and final concept in our search for effectiveness and excellence.

SECTION FIVE

FAITH: "I'm Just an Old Chunk of Coal, But I'm Gonna Be a Diamond Someday."

"So that your trust may be in the Lord,
I teach you today, even you."—Proverbs 22:19

Chapter Twenty-Two

"We'll Be Back"

By this time, you're either fired up and ready to mission-ize, strategize, and organize, or you're about ready to give up. In either case, this last section is designed to provide one final tool you'll need if you're going to mine the gold that's in your life.

As I mentioned in the Introduction, I often came away from seminars or books on time management more burdened than when I began. I didn't see how I could possibly do more, and I felt guilty and under pressure. I realized that the one element missing in these presentations was what this section addresses—faith in God.

It's quite possible for you to have read the first four sections and dismiss them as things that apply to someone else. This section, however, pertains to you and every believer. If you don't apply anything else you've read, you need to pay attention to this section and make it part of your life.

Perhaps you find yourself where many people are: You believe that God can do great things in general, but you're not totally convinced that He can do great things with and through you. Maybe you're painfully aware of your past failures and inadequacies, and those things are weighing you down. You may have even tried some of the things discussed in the previous sections, such as to-do lists and goals, but found no lasting success in implementing them. Even if you did find your purpose, set goals, and become more organized, you may be thinking that you still wouldn't be able to do great things for the Lord.

That's why this section is subtitled, "I'm Just an Old Chunk of Coal, But I'm Gonna Be a Diamond Someday." That comes from a country-western song sung years ago by John Anderson, and it summarizes the mind-set you must have if the Lord is to use you for His glory. Abraham, Sarah, Joseph, Moses, David, Esther, Daniel, and Jesus' disciples all started out as "chunks of coal"— raw material in the hand of the Lord. James wrote, "Elijah was a man just like us. He prayed earnestly that it would not rain, and it did not rain on the land for three and a half years" (James 5:17). The prophet Elijah was just like you and me, yet God used him to bring a great deliverance in Israel.

Through the same process that makes diamonds from coal— heat, pressure, and time—these men and women of God became precious. They were transformed from ordinary people into extraordinary champions, leaving a legacy for others to follow for thousands of years. When you come right down to it, you're no different from them. The key element in their transformation wasn't a mission statement, a goal sheet, or an industrial-size planner. The key element was *their faith in God.*

The coal-to-diamonds mentality says, "This is where I am today, but this isn't where I'll be tomorrow," and "God isn't finished with me yet." Coal-to-diamonds faith means that, regardless of how it looks today or how many failures there were yesterday, you've learned to trust, not in your own abilities to make things happen, but in God's ability.

Covey says the second habit of effective people is "Begin with the end in mind." He writes,

> The most fundamental application of "begin with the end in mind" is to begin today with the image, picture, or paradigm of the end of your life as your frame of reference or the criterion by which everything else is examined. . . .By keeping that end clearly in mind, you can make certain that whatever you do on any particular day does not violate the criteria you have defined as supremely important.[1]

The "end in mind" for you is that God isn't finished with you yet. You should be able to focus on the end and keep it before you so that it will guide how you live and what you say. You can do this through faith that God will finish the work He began in you.

The coal-to-diamonds mentality is the same mentality that

Abraham had on Mt. Moriah. He had been instructed to go there by an angel of the Lord and, once there, to sacrifice his son, Isaac. Isaac was the son of promise; Abraham had pinned his hopes for the future on him. But Abraham obediently went to the place the Lord had shown him.

Once he arrived, he spoke these amazing words to his servants who had traveled with him: "Stay here with the donkey while I and the boy go over there. We will worship and *then we will come back to you*" (Genesis 22:5, emphasis added). As far as Abraham was concerned, he was going up that mountain to sacrifice his son. Yet he trusted that God would return that son to him because Isaac was God's promise to Abraham. He said, *"We'll* be back," and not *"I'll* be back."

No wonder Abraham is the father of the faithful. He had "we'll-be-back" faith. When it seemed hopeless and he couldn't see his way out, he said, "We'll be back." He didn't ask the servants to pray for him; he didn't seek sympathy or give room for self pity. He simply said, "We'll be back." In Abraham's mind, he had already sacrificed Isaac; Isaac was dead to him. That's why the writer of Hebrews wrote, "Abraham reasoned that God could raise the dead, and figuratively speaking, he did receive Isaac back from death" (Hebrews 11:19).

If you're Abraham's child, then you need "we'll-be-back" faith, keeping the end in mind, in order to mine your gold. You may have failed at business or ministry before; there may be broken relationships in your past; your financial track record may not be the best. In other words, you may be just an old chunk of coal. But "we'll-be-back" faith says that you'll be a diamond someday through the grace and power of God. Keeping that in mind will cause you to act according to what the end will be and not what today says.

Romans 14:23 states, "Everything that does not come from faith is sin." I looked up the Greek word for "everything" and made a startling discovery. The word for "everything" in that verse means "everything." Isn't that profound? There are no exceptions. Your purpose, goals, time management, and organization must start from and be sustained by your faith. If not, they represent your own efforts and will fade away just as every fad or burst of human energy eventually does.

Hebrews 11:6 says, "It's impossible to please God." There's

nothing you can say that He doesn't already know; there's nothing you can do that He hasn't seen before or done better; there's nothing you can give Him that He needs; nor is there anything you can create that would impress Him. "It's impossible to please God."

Thank God that's not all the verse has to say. In its entirety, it says, "Without faith, it's impossible to please God." Without faith, God is not moved. With it, men and women, some of whom are listed in Hebrews 11, did great things and pleased the Lord in the process.

The most striking thing to me about those people listed in Hebrews 11 is their humanity. None of them was perfect, and some of them had severe character flaws. Yet they operated in faith, and the Lord was pleased with them, so much so that He showcased their lives in this faith "hall of fame" chapter of the Bible.

Think of it. Could Samson (a man with moral problems) be a member in some churches today, let alone a leader? Could Rahab (a prostitute) head up the ladies' prayer meeting? Could Moses (a murderer) lead a denomination today? And how about King David after his adultery and attempted cover-up? Would he have remained king after the modern media had torn him apart through investigative reporting?

In each case, God did not present these heroes for their short-comings; they were put forth as examples because they were men and women of faith. It was their faith that made the difference, and your faith will make the difference as well.

Faith is critical because it takes you from the realm of the seen to the realm of the unseen. When you exercise faith, it puts you in touch with reality—not the reality of the five senses, but the reality of the heavenly realm. Faith opens your ears to hear and your eyes to see things from God's perspective, thus freeing you from the limited perspective of this world. Faith also enables you to say, "We'll be back" just like Abraham did.

Paul wrote, "So we fix our eyes not on what is seen, but on what is unseen. For what is seen is temporary, but what is unseen is eternal" (2 Corinthians 4:18). In the next chapter, we'll examine this principle in the life of the prophet Elisha, and then proceed from there to offer suggestions on how to apply your faith in everyday life.

Chapter Twenty-Three

Ears That Hear, Eyes That See

As you know by now, I love the book of Proverbs. Just like other books in the Bible, some of the verses in Proverbs are harder to comprehend than others. One such verse for me is found in Proverbs 20:12: "Ears that hear, and eyes that see—the Lord has made them both."

For years I wondered what that meant. Common sense told me that the Lord is the Creator of all, including my eyes and ears. And common sense further told me that He made them to see and hear respectively. Why would the writer of Proverbs sense a need to write this seemingly simple and obvious verse?

As I've studied and meditated on this, I've come to realize some of what Proverbs 20:12 is all about. To help explain it to you, I will use a story found in 2 Kings 6.

Now the King of Aram was at war with Israel. After conferring with his officers, he said, "I will set up my camp in such and such a place." The man of God sent word to the king of Israel: "Beware of passing that place, because the Arameans are going down there." So the King of Israel checked on the place indicated by the man of God. Time and again Elisha warned the king, so that he was on his guard in such places. This enraged the King of Aram. He summoned his officers and demanded of them, "Will you not tell me which of us is on the side of the king of Israel?" "None of us, my lord the king," said one of his officers, "but Elisha, the prophet who is in Israel, tells the king of Israel the very words you speak in your bedroom" (verses 8-12).

The only logical answer for the king of Aram was that there

was a spy in his midst. Someone was leaking information to the press, so to speak, because the king of Israel always knew what the king of Aram was about to do.

There was a spiritual reason, however, behind the king's predicament. There was a man in Israel who had "ears to hear." Elisha didn't pay attention to what everyone else was hearing; he listened to the voice of the Lord. Elisha was using his ears to hear what they were created to hear.

What about you? What do you allow your ears to hear? Do you hear the economic reports and then decide that this isn't a good time to give, invest, or build? When you set your goals, do you let someone else tell you how it can't be done or why you aren't the one to do it? If so, that's not what God made your ears for. He made them to hear His voice and, when you hear it, to march to the beat of His drum.

The story goes on.

"Go, find out where he is," the king ordered, "so I can send men and capture him." The report came back: "He is in Dothan." Then he sent horses and chariots and a strong force there. They went by night and surrounded the city (2 Kings 6:13-14).

This shows the foolishness of the king of Aram's natural mind! He was just told that the prophet always knew what the king was planning, so the king turned around and contrived another plan as before. What made him think that the prophet didn't know about this most recent plot?

When the servant of the man of God got up and went out early the next morning, an army with chariots and horses had sur-rounded the city. "Oh, my lord, what shall we do?" the servant asked (2 Kings 6:15).

Maybe that's your cry as you read this: "Oh, my Lord, the rent is due next Saturday. What shall we do?" "Oh, my Lord. How can I afford a computer?" "Oh, my Lord. Where will the money come from for the ministry or business?" "Lord, how can I find the time to finish school and work full-time?"

If so, then the Lord would say the same thing to you that He said through the prophet to his servant. "'Don't be afraid,' the prophet answered. 'Those who are with us are more than those who are with them'" (2 Kings 6:16). Perhaps the servant thought, "He doesn't know the situation. I've seen it with my own eyes and it's bad. Let's call the Pentagon or the National Guard. My master has his head in the clouds. He doesn't understand."

Maybe you've done the same thing. Someone has tried to encourage you that your financial situation isn't as bad as you think, yet you've responded with the same words. Perhaps someone has told you that you need a church building, but you know how hard it is to get real estate in your area. Or maybe you've had the idea of opening your own business, but there is "no way" you see to get it started. Even though all those answers may be true, your circumstances don't necessarily need to change. *You* may need to change and use your eyes for their God-given purpose.

And Elisha prayed, "Oh, Lord, open his eyes so he may see." Then the Lord opened the servant's eyes, and he looked and saw the hills full of horses and chariots of fire all around Elisha (2 Kings 6:17).

Notice that none of the circumstances changed after Elisha prayed. The foreign armies didn't leave, nor did another army arrive to help. The servant didn't arm himself, nor did bad weather chase the invaders away. The only thing that happened was that the servant's eyes were opened. The prophet understood that the only thing that needed to take place was for his servant's eyes to be opened.

Gold Nugget Twenty

"Open your eyes, and you will be satisfied with food."
—Proverbs 20:13 (NAS)

Covey writes a great deal about the concept of paradigms (pronounced pair-a-*dimes*). "A simple way to understand paradigms is to see them as maps.... [A paradigm] is a theory, an explanation, or model of something else."[2] Covey goes on to explain that "to try to change outward attitudes and behaviors does very little good in the long run if we fail to examine the basic paradigms from which those attitudes and behaviors flow."[3]

For instance, prior to Christopher Columbus, most people held the paradigm that the world was flat. Artists drew sketches of ships sailing off the end of the world, and these sketches were consistent with and reinforced the paradigm of the day. A contemporary of the flat-earth paradigm was the one that believed the planets revolved around the earth rather than the sun.

Columbus caused a paradigm shift when he sailed to the new world and proved the earth to be round. Copernicus made possible a paradigm shift when he proved the sun to be at the center of the universe as it truly is. People continued to fight the reality of the new paradigms, but their resistance didn't stop the paradigm shifts from taking place.

When you see with eyes of faith, your paradigm or model for reality changes. Elisha's servant experienced a paradigm shift when he saw the chariots and horses that surrounded the army of Aram. You, too, may need only a paradigm shift rather than a change in your circumstances.

Paul wrote to the Ephesian church,

I pray also that the eyes of your heart may be enlightened *in order that you may know the hope to which he has called you, the riches of his glorious inheritance in the saints, and his incomparably great power for us who believe* (Ephesians 1:18-19, emphasis added).

Paul knew what Elisha had known centuries before Paul ever ministered: God wants His people to see things from His perspective. He wants to shift their paradigm from what can be seen with the eyes to the paradigm that comes from the unseen. When they do and begin to trust in that eternal perspective, they have understanding that God can empower them to do great things, regardless of what it looks like in the natural.

Consider this fact in the lives of those mentioned in Hebrews 11 by looking at the following verses:

1. *"Now faith is being sure of what we hope for and certain of what we do not see"* (11:1). The essence of faith is to be certain not

of what you can see but of what you can't see. Enlightened eyes provide certainty about those things that can't be seen with the natural mind.

2. *"By faith we understand that the universe was formed at God's command, so that what is seen was not made out of what was visible"* (11:3). The source for what is seen is not found in other raw materials that can also be seen. The root of what is seen is in the invisible word of God that brought forth creation.

3. *"By faith Noah, when warned about things not yet seen..."* (11:7). God spoke to Noah about rain, floods, and an ark, all things that had never been seen before in the natural. Noah put his faith in God's word, even though he had no historical precedent for what the Lord said.[4]

4. *"For he was looking forward to the city with foundations"* (11:10). What caused Abraham to leave his country and set out for parts unknown? He saw another city, built by God. With that firmly in sight, he set out on a journey that changed the course of mankind.

5. *"All these people were still living by faith when they died. They did not receive the things promised; they only saw them and welcomed them"* (11:13). The people of old saw the promises and welcomed them. They didn't actually see them come to pass in history, but when they saw them with their spiritual sight, they felt as if they had them already. They died "in faith" because of what they saw, and God was pleased with them. Seeing things from an eternal perspective in the absence of time may bring the reality of those things much closer than they really are. Yet that doesn't make them any less real.

6. *"By faith Moses' parents hid him for three months after he was born, because they saw he was no ordinary child"* (11:23). When our son was born, my wife looked at him and said, "Maybe he'll be intelligent." No newborn is beautiful at first due to the trauma of birth. Moses' parents looked at this boy and ignored Pharaoh's edict that he be thrown into the river. They saw the pur-

pose of God on him and it caused them to act differently than the other parents of the day.

7. *"He [Moses] was looking ahead to his reward"* (11:26). Moses turned his back on his Egyptian inheritance because he saw something else: the reward for the people of God, which was ultimately the Messiah.

8. *"By faith he left Egypt, not fearing the king's anger; he persevered because he saw him who is invisible"* (11:27). Pharaoh was in Moses' face, threatening him with threats he could back up with all the power of the Egyptian army. Moses looked right past the one he could see (Pharaoh) to One who can't be seen (the Lord). What he saw in the invisible allowed him to act and eventually pull down the military power of Egypt without an arrow being shot.

9. *"Let us fix our eyes on Jesus, the author and perfecter of our faith"* (12:2). You are commanded to fix your eyes on the One who is invisible. If you can do that, you will find the source and sustainer of your faith. If you focus on circumstances, your faith will lose its lifeline and perish.

Let me illustrate this further from my own personal experience. In 1984, we put our house up for sale, but for months nothing happened. We decided that faith requires action (something we will discuss later), so we went out and looked for a new house before the old house was sold. To our surprise, the first house we looked at was the one we fell in love with.

We went home content that we had found our new house, but still nothing was happening on the sale of our old home. So we decided that the next thing to do was to put an offer on the new house, contingent on the sale of our old one.

In the meantime, a family from India submitted an offer on the old home that was so low, we rejected it outright with no counter offer. We were approaching the deadline on the deal, and I prayed one morning and asked God to open my eyes so that I could see what I was missing. That evening my daughter, then just four years old, came running in to tell me that the "Indian family" had just driven by our house. When she said that, I knew that my prayer had been answered. At that very instant, the Lord opened my eyes to see that the people who had submitted the only offer we had received were still interested. I had rejected their offer because I thought it was too low. I realized then and there that I was to take their offer and trust the Lord for the money we would still need to move into our new home.

I called my realtor that night and told him to make the best deal he could. Just 36 hours before our deadline on the new house offer, we sold our house. Of course, we were still $10,000 short of what we needed to close on the new home. God had opened my eyes, however, and I was trusting Him.

Two weeks later, we closed on that new house. Someone unexpectedly loaned us the $10,000 at a low interest rate. We paid that money back and enjoyed our new home for five years, selling it after we relocated to Orlando, Florida. The Lord had used my four- year-old to open my eyes and I saw things from His perspective. The rest was worked out in the natural as I relied on Him for the provision.

God will do the same for you. He wants you to have eyes that see and ears that hear, just as He created them. As we close this chapter, let's touch on one more verse. Perhaps you've quoted it or heard someone preach about it. It's found in Ephesians 3:20 and is most often quoted, "Now to him who is able to do immeasurably more than all we ask or imagine." If you've ever quoted that verse in that way, you've made a serious mistake! God is not able to do immeasurably more than all you ask or imagine because He is not in the "immeasurably-more" business without having the last part of that verse included, "according to his power that is at work within us." If there's no power working in you, then God's power is limited, not by design, but by His choice.

What energizes the power within you? It's the vision you have of what God can do that comes when you use your eyes to see and ears to hear. That vision of the "end in mind" allows you to trust the Lord to do what He said or showed you He would do, regardless of what is happening around you. God is faithful and powerful, but your faith in Him releases His power to act on your behalf.

Gold Nugget Twenty-One

"Where there is no vision, the people are unrestrained."
—Proverbs 29:18 (NAS)

Before you read the next chapter, ask the Lord to open your ears and eyes. Ask Him to show you what you haven't seen that can make the difference in your life. Maybe you need to stop praying for your situation to change, and start praying for your heart to change. Or maybe you just need to have your eyes or ears opened. Perhaps you can't see yourself fulfilling your purpose or achieving lofty goals. You may be saying, "I'm disorganized and that's how I'll always be." If so, then you need to change your paradigm.

There's no better way to change your heart or paradigm than to clarify your vision of reality from the Lord's perspective. Once you've done that, move on to the next chapter that will show you how to preserve your faith so that you can see the object of your faith fulfilled.

Chapter Twenty-Four

How Can I Be Sure?

There was a pop song out years ago by a group called The Little Rascals with the opening line, "How can I be sure? In a world that's constantly changing, how can I be sure, where I stand with you?"* And that's the question I'm most often asked when it comes to operating in faith: How can I be sure it's the Lord so that I'm not walking in presumption?

You may be concerned because you've seen others so sure they were walking in faith, only to be disappointed when what they had faith for never came to pass. Those stories may have prevented you from acting in bold faith because you had a fear of ending up like the disappointed people.

I've had to work through that issue myself, for as a pastor, I saw my share of faith adventures gone awry. And to be truthful, I've had a few myself. Yet over the years I've answered two related questions that have helped me answer the question, "How can I be sure?"

A fellow pastor asked me the first question while we were having lunch. He asked me, "Why do you think there are counterfeit $20 bills?" I thought for a while but couldn't give him a satisfactory answer. He finally answered his own question by saying, "Because there are real $20 bills." No one is going to go to the trouble of counterfeiting something that has no value. Counterfeiters imitate the real thing in hopes of passing off the fake as real.

Just because I know there are counterfeit $20 bills doesn't mean I refuse to accept any $20 bills at all. If I'm that concerned about getting a fake $20, I would simply take precautions to make sure that what I get is real. If a phony bill were to get by me, I would accept it as loss and try to be more careful. But if I became so paranoid that what I'm getting may be fake, I could pass up the real thing by being too cautious.

That's how it is with faith. Of course there is counterfeit faith in circulation. It's there to discourage the people of God from operating in real and vibrant faith. Just because some (even you) have accepted a fake at one time or another doesn't mean that you should reject all faith. Treat the mistakes like you would treat that fake $20 bill: Learn from it and be better prepared to distinguish the real from the fake.

Answering that question helped me see that there are no sure things in life or faith. I saw that my desire to know for sure before I would ever act was unrealistic and presumptuous. Abraham didn't understand it all before he left his homeland, and once he started, he made some mistakes along the way. Fortunately, he didn't give up on ever having an Isaac just because he had fathered an Ishmael. God is bigger than my mistakes, and is able to work with my mistakes if my heart is right.

The second question that helped me answer "How can I be sure?" was asked by a fellow pastor in a message on the family. He challenged me, "Because there's divorce, do you stop holding out marriage as God's standard for the family?" After some thought, I concluded the answer was "no." I've seen some marriages end in divorce, yet I've continued to give marriage counseling, perform weddings, and do all I could to uphold the family. I've mourned the divorces, but I haven't given up on marriage.

I concluded that's how you should also treat faith. Just because imperfect people have applied it imperfectly at times doesn't mean that you should be afraid or hesitant to walk in faith yourself. Hold onto the truth that "without faith it's impossible to please God" and walk in it, knowing that you are imperfect and will never have perfect knowledge or understanding.

With that in mind, you won't be shocked or allow your faith to be shipwrecked when having to make mid-course changes or adjustments if you understand the Lord and your own motives more clearly. In other words, you'll be like the father who told Jesus, "I do believe; help me overcome my unbelief" (Mark 9:24).

This father admitted his imperfection, including his unbelief, and Jesus *still* healed his boy. His unbelief didn't cause the Lord to shun him or leave him until his faith was perfect. Instead, the man's honest admission of his human weakness still moved the Lord to act on his behalf.

While there is always the danger that you're moving in your own strength or understanding, there are two things that will help you avoid the pain of faith that is presumptuous or off course. These two things can also help you answer the question, "How can I be sure?" The first is to realize that *the agenda for your faith rests in God's hands.* The second is that *you must prepare your heart to receive the word of the Lord*, the foundation for your faith. Let's address both these issues separately.

The agenda for your faith rests in God, so you don't have to work up one for yourself. You don't have to ask, "What will I believe the Lord for today?" This also means that you aren't free to decide what you want to have, what you want to be, and how you want to get there. All those things should have their beginning in the Lord, and you should enter into their reality after He has made them clear to you.

And that's good news. God is the initiator or author of your faith. It's not up to you to work up or work out your faith. God has given each person a measure of faith, and He will show you where you need to exercise that faith. When God wants to make something clear, He is more than able to do it. All you have to be is receptive and willing to follow through.

On May 18, 1973, I met the Lord through a simple but profound conversion. Having been Catholic, I had studied to be a priest for five years before leaving to pursue other interests. On May 19, I knew that the Lord was saying to me, "You're going to leave your church, go into full-time ministry and preach, and give your life to My service."

How did I know? I'm not sure. That's not something I really wanted to do, nor was it something I was anticipating. But I couldn't shake that truth from that day on. God had communicated with me, and it was up to me to put my faith in what He showed me that day. The ministry became part of my faith agenda. How sure was I? I was certain that the Lord had spoken to me. Did I have times of doubt? Definitely! During those times, all I could do was put my faith in what I believed I had heard from the Lord. The rest was up to Him.

Others who have been called to the ministry can share their own callings, and some are certainly more dramatic than mine. My point is that I placed my faith in that call and hung onto it through good times and bad. And there were plenty of bad times.

I didn't step into my own pulpit until 16 years later. There were times when I was so far away from a pulpit that I didn't see how the gap could ever be closed. All I had was that word from the Lord. And there were times during those 16 years when I hoped that it *wouldn't* come true. But every time I would get low, the Lord would send a messenger, a verse, or a reminder, and His promise would be activated in me once again—I would one day be in His service.

This is the same situation in which Abraham found himself. While he wanted a child, it was the Lord who had initiated the promise of a son. Abraham didn't make that up; God spoke it to him.

There were times when it seemed like the promise had failed. Abraham had even tried to assist God by getting Sarah's maid pregnant. Even in the midst of his failure, however, the word remained in effect. Then, when Abraham was 100 years old, the word of the Lord came true, and he had a son.

Abraham didn't "name and claim" a child. He didn't decide one day that the Lord owed him a son because he saw so many others who had one or more. You don't ever have to do that, either. God spoke to Abraham, and that became the foundation for his faith that he would have a son. God will speak to you, too, and your only responsibility is to hear and obey. Abraham's faith agenda began and ended with God. Yours does too as you trust in Jesus, "the author and perfecter of our faith."

Now when I say that the Lord will speak to you, you may again be concerned how God will speak, and whether you'll be able to hear. Don't worry. God is able to make clear whatever He wants to say. He may use circumstances, another person, a verse of Scripture, that still, small inner voice, or any combination of these to confirm His word for your life. Even then you may have doubt. What better time to exercise what faith you do have!

Having established that the Lord will set your faith agenda, the second issue you must address (if you are to know for sure) is that you must prepare your heart to receive God's word. Faith doesn't have to be dramatic with lightning flashes and the voice of God blasting from the mountaintop. Faith can and often does come as you prepare your heart, a heart that is often ill-equipped to do business with God.

When my wife and I were first married, we considered a verse in Exodus that says,

> *If you listen carefully to the voice of the Lord your God and do what is right in his eyes, if you pay attention to his commands and keep all his decrees, I will not bring on you any of the diseases I brought on the Egyptians, for I am the Lord, who heals you* (Exodus 15:26).

We talked about that verse and "chewed" on it. We wondered if the diseases of Egypt meant chickenpox, measles, and the like. After deliberating for quite a while, we decided that it must and accepted that promise for our children. I can remember praying together and thanking the Lord for making that promise real to us. Our grown children have never had the chickenpox. There were 17 children in our son John's kindergarten class, and 16 got chickenpox. John was the only exception.

I've never preached that verse or subject, nor have I "put" that verse on anyone else. My wife and I were convinced that this was true, but we believe that the Lord was the one who drew our attention to that verse and then made it real in our lives. I'm not going to browbeat anyone else to accept it for their children. We tried to prepare our hearts to receive that word and the Lord did the rest.

The writer of Hebrews included this admonition:

> *So, as the Holy Spirit says: "Today, if you hear his voice, do not harden your hearts as you did in the rebellion, during the time of testing in the desert, where your fathers tested and tried me and for forty years saw what I did. That is why I was angry with that generation, and I said, 'Their hearts are always going astray, and they have not known my ways.' So I declared on oath in my anger, 'They shall never enter my rest.'"* See to it, brothers, that none of you has a sinful, unbelieving heart that turns away from the living God (Hebrews 3:7-12, emphasis added).

176

The writer didn't suggest that the people not have a "sinful, unbelieving heart." He *commanded* them not to allow one to develop. And it seems that the writer especially cautioned you to be careful not to harden your heart "if you hear his voice." When the Lord speaks, you can choose to accept and act, or to ignore and stay put. The decision is yours; very often that decision will be dictated by the condition of our heart.

There are many ways to keep your heart in good shape. Maintain a vibrant prayer life; read the Word of God regularly and with understanding. Choose topics and study what the word of God has to say about them in depth. Memorizing Scripture verses is a good way to store the Word in your heart.

I also carry with me a brief journal of significant things the Lord has shown me over the years. I refer to this list in times of discouragement, and it refreshes me by allowing me to remember truths the Lord has shown me from His Word or through experience. There are others who have made a practice of keeping a daily journal that chronicles their walk with the Lord. Every now and then they read their journal entries, which reminds them of the Lord's faithfulness and stimulates their faith.

You may also want to consider keeping your own journal, using your time-management system or your computer for regular entries. But at least have a file or some other means to maintain those special words that the Lord has given you.

I've found fasting to be an excellent practice that helps keep your heart soft and pliable in God's hands. You may want to choose a regular day on which you fast and also block out on your calendar several days every six months or so when you just give up eating and spend that time with the Lord.

Finally, asking the Lord to show you the condition of your heart should be a regular prayer. The psalmist wrote, "Search me, O God, and know my heart; test me and know my anxious thoughts. See if there is any offensive way in me, and lead me in the way everlasting" (Psalm 139:23-24). God knows the condition of your heart, and can keep you aware of what's there as well. The key is to ask Him to do so.

When it comes to faith, everyone must answer the question, "How can I be sure?" While you can never be 100% certain, there are steps you can take to make your margin for error smaller and smaller as you walk in faith. First of all, *relax.* Jesus is the author and initiator of your faith. Then *prepare your heart* to receive the word of the Lord and work to keep it from hardening once you've heard. If you *make your best efforts*, God won't abandon you. He'll meet you where you are because anyone who comes to Him "must believe that he exists and that he rewards those who earnestly seek him" (Hebrews 11:6). With that in mind, let's move on to define the final steps to be taken if you're to make the transition from coal to diamonds.

Chapter Twenty-Five

Walk in What You See

Faith takes you from the realm of the seen to the realm of the unseen. It causes you to walk and act according to invisible circumstances that sometimes would seem to warrant doing the exact opposite of what you can see would dictate. If the bills are due and you have a few dollars, the last thing you should do in the natural is to give that money away. Yet, when you move from the realm of the seen to the unseen, that may be the very thing you need to do.

You may feel that you must deny reality, not even mentioning what is happening around you, if you are to have your faith rewarded. This has led some people to deny symptoms of sickness, ignore financial problems, or make desperate faith confessions to try to escape difficult situations. But walking in what you see in the invisible doesn't require you to do any of that.

Gold Nugget Twenty-Two

"A fool's eyes wander to the ends of the earth."
— Proverbs 17:24

Paul wrote about Abraham in the epistle to the Romans, describing Abraham's struggle in becoming a father. He wrote,

Against all hope, Abraham in hope believed and so became the father of many nations, just as it had been said to him, "So shall your offspring be." Without weakening in his faith, he faced the fact that his body was as good as dead—since he was about a hundred years old—and that Sarah's womb was also dead. Yet

he did not waver through unbelief regarding the promise of God,
but was strengthened in his faith and gave glory to God, being
fully persuaded that God had power to do what he had promised.
This is why "it was credited to him as righteousness" (Romans
4:18-22).

Abraham didn't deny the reality of his situation. His body was
dead and so was Sarah's. He didn't tell people that he was alive,
that in faith he was as good as a 20-year old. Abraham said, "I'm
dead."

But Abraham is our father in the faith because he didn't stop
there. He chose to focus on the unseen promise of God without
wavering. If someone asked Abraham, "How are you going to
have a son?" He probably replied, "I don't know. I'm dead, but
God's alive. And if He's alive, then anything can happen." He
didn't make silly statements trying to prove to people that he and
Sarah still had some supernatural ability to produce a child. He
faced the facts—he was dead. He lived in a more powerful fact,
however. God was able to do what He had promised, and that
saved the day.

I've referred throughout this book to my 16-year wait for a
pulpit. I didn't use those 16 years applying for a pulpit position or
maneuvering to get a chance to preach. God had me boxed in, and
there was nowhere to go. But I didn't waste those years. I used
them by walking in the greater truth that God had shown me—I
was a preacher, and one day, regardless of what it seemed like, I
would preach.

So I used those years to get ready. I studied as many preachers
as I could. I wrote my own sermons and then preached to myself
in the car. I preached to my kids, my wife, my home group (which
sometimes numbered four people, including my wife and me), and
the canary.

While I wasn't preaching, I would visualize myself preaching.
In my mind, I worked out a preaching style and philosophy that
helped me discover what I would say and how I would say it
when I got the chance.

Covey refers to this ability to visualize when he writes,

Through imagination, we can visualize the uncreated

worlds of potential that lie within us. Through conscience, we can come in contact with universal laws or principles with our own singular talents and avenues of contribution, and with the personal guidelines within which we can most effectively develop them. Combined with self-aware-ness, these two endowments empower us to write our own script. Because we already live with many scripts that have been handed to us, the process of writing our own script is actually more a process of "rescripting" or para-digm shifting.[5]

I did what Covey writes about. I visualized my "uncreated world of potential" to preach, and it helped prepare me for the day when it was no longer just potential. I stress that this potential didn't come from my talent or a decision to be a preacher. This "world of potential" came from the Lord who called me and then empowered me to fulfill it. (However, when Covey refers to this "world" apart from a divine endowment, it concerns me that he is referring to an innate goodness or potential that man has on his own to succeed.)

My paradigm for this concept is this: God is my source for all good things. Paul, a great missionary, preacher, theologian, and writer, told the Galatians, "I have been crucified with Christ and I no longer live, but Christ lives in me. The life I live in the body, I live by faith in the Son of God, who loved me and gave himself for me" (Galatians 2:20). Paul didn't see any untapped potential in his inner man. He had died, and the life and success he enjoyed came from Christ, who lived in him.

When the call came for me to pastor a church, I was ready be-cause I had walked in the reality of the unseen. I chose (and some-times forced myself) to ignore circumstances and prepare according to God's agenda. I held the paradigm that God's word made me a preacher, whether I was preaching at that particular season in my life or not.

When I finally "arrived," I had material ready to preach and knew what kind of preacher I wanted to be. When my call reached its fulfillment, I was glad I had prepared myself according to the vision I had of the unseen and not according to the "reality" of my current circumstances.

I've briefly touched on how faith affects your speech; this is a good time to address that more fully. The book of Proverbs has plenty of verses that speak about the tongue. James' epistle, sometimes called the Proverbs of the New Testament, also has much to say about your speech. You may be asking yourself, "What is appropriate to say when I'm walking in faith and everything around me seems to make my faith foolish?" At times like that, you simply say what the Lord has already said or shown you. And if you don't know what to say, don't say anything.

For instance, when people would ask me what I felt God had called me to do before I ever went to pastor the church, I would tell them "to preach." They would then ask me all the normal questions: Where are you preaching now? Did you go to seminary? If you're not preaching, why aren't you? Shouldn't you get a pulpit somewhere?

I would reply that the Lord had called me to preach and that He would open a place for me. I further explained that I had never applied for a job in my life and didn't feel that I should start applying for a church position. I was where God had me for that season, and I was content to be there. Beyond that, there wasn't much else I could say. Some didn't understand, but I kept right on saying that God had called me to preach, because He had. Just because I wasn't preaching at the time didn't negate that fact.

Gold Nugget Twenty-Three

"From the fruit of his mouth a man's stomach is filled;
with the harvest from his lips he is satisfied. The tongue has the
power of life and death, and those who love it will eat its fruit."
—Proverbs 18:20-21

I'm sure some didn't understand either when Abram changed his name. Can you picture this fictitious scene at the name-change bureau? Abram, whose name meant "exalted father," came to the clerk and announced his intent to change his name. When the clerk asked him what his new name would be, he announced it to be Abraham, which means "father of a multitude."

Intrigued by such a name change, maybe the clerk asked Abraham a logical question: "How many children do you have?" to which Abraham had to respond, "None!" At that point, the clerk probably just rolled his eyes and wondered what kind of religious "kook" he was dealing with, who would change his name to "father of a multitude" though he was old and without children.

The point is that Abraham changed his name, not because he decided to do so, but because the Lord *told* him to do it. God wanted Abraham and everyone around him to make a faith statement each time they said that name. There are times when you can and must say what you know to be true, *not to try to make something happen*, but to acknowledge that in God's time something will happen.

Because they were people of faith, those mentioned in Hebrews 11 had seen only by faith what they proclaimed. For instance, "By faith Jacob, when he was dying, blessed each of Joseph's sons" (Hebrews 11:21) even though he died in Egypt. It's written about Joseph that "when his end was near, [he] spoke about the exodus of the Israelites from Egypt and gave instructions about his bones" (Hebrews 11:22). Both Jacob and Joseph acknowledged the fact that their people would return to their land someday by making a faith confession. God had said it and they could, too.

Paul referred to this same principle when he wrote, "It is written: 'I believed, therefore I have spoken.' With that same spirit of faith, we also believe and therefore speak" (2 Corinthians 4:13). What is it that you believe and, because you do, can't keep to yourself?

And finally, when you are firm in what you have seen, it's then time to take action. James wrote, "Faith by itself, if it is not accompanied by action, is dead" (James 2:17). Faith is more than adhering to a correct doctrine. The demons believe in the Trinity, beholding it regularly, but that fact hasn't changed them one bit.

You must shift any paradigm you're holding that says your faith is what you believe doctrinally. Your faith *must* translate into action or it's not faith at all. It's not giving mental assent to the doctrine of the Trinity that makes you a Christian. It's what you do because of your faith in the Trinity that makes you a Christian.

In an earlier chapter, I told of our adventure in purchasing a new home before we ever sold our old home. I had to ask myself each step of the way, "What can I *do* at this moment? What can I do so that I've done all I can, leaving the rest up to the Lord?"

My faith that I would one day preach also required me to do

something. I chose to get ready to preach as opposed to applying for associate pastor positions. My point is that faith always leads to action. Not one hero of the faith in Hebrews 11 was a great theologian. Instead, each one knew how to act on his or her faith. Let's look at the people mentioned in that chapter and see how they acted on their faith to God.

Abel	offered a better sacrifice
Noah	built an ark
Abraham	left his home, made a home in a new place, offered Isaac
Isaac	blessed Jacob and Esau
Jacob	blessed his sons and worshiped God
Joseph	gave instructions about his bones
Moses	left Egypt and kept the Passover
Israel	passed through the Red Sea; marched and the walls fell
Rahab	hid the spies

In addition, we are told that other people…

…through faith conquered kingdoms, administered justice, and gained what was promised; who shut the mouths of lions, quenched the fury of the flames, and escaped the edge of the sword; whose weakness was turned to strength; and who became powerful in battle and routed foreign armies (Hebrews 11:33-34).

Faith requires action and those who took action in faith are mentioned and honored in the Word of God in spite of their weakness and sin. Those who move in faith are still honored by the Lord, and He works with and through them in spite of their weakness and failure.

I'm not only talking about faith for your car payment, shoes for your children, and a roof over your head—the necessities of life. I'm talking about faith to fulfill the Great Commission, from which the Church is to disciple the nations. How can you have faith for Africa or Asia if you can't exercise faith for the simple things? How will you trust the Lord for the millions of dollars it will take to publish Bibles in the thousands of dialects currently without the Word of God if you can't trust Him for the $25 monthly commitment you've made to help support your church's missionary to India?

If you believe in Jesus' resurrection, and I'm sure you do, then you're in for an adventure! Anyone who has faith to believe that God took a three-day-old dead body and infused it with life can have faith for anything! The same Spirit that raised a dead man back to life dwells in you, helping you in ways you can't see or understand. He's there in you, and together you can do great things.

With that fact established, you can find and accomplish your purpose. In faith, you can set goals and in faith you can see them fulfilled "beyond all you can ask or think." Like Joshua, you can have faith that God will help you maximize your use of time and help you to do more with the time you have. You can take your faith to your desk, garage, or kitchen and trust the Lord to show you how to organize it and keep it ordered.

John wrote his first epistle and penned these words:

For everyone born of God overcomes the world. This is the victory that has overcome the world, even our faith. Who is it that overcomes the world? Only he who believes that Jesus is the Son of God (1 John 5:4-5).

You can overcome the world and its obstacles through faith. Someone wrote, "It's not the greatness of my faith that moves mountains, but my faith in the greatness of God." With that in mind, move on to the last chapter where you'll find some practical assignments to further help you walk in faith that will please God and perhaps change the world.

Chapter Twenty-Six

"Action!"

So now that you've decided to walk according to the unseen and act on your faith, where can you go from here? To give you some direction, I've included a few activities that have nurtured my faith over the years. I offer them to you in hopes that they will spur you to love and good deeds as the Bible commands.

1. Is your giving all it can be?

If you keep financial records, check to see what percentage of your income you gave away last year. Are you satisfied with that amount? If not, what percent would you like to give away this year? When you decide that, then determine how much you must give away each month to achieve that percentage. I've found that my giving is the most practical and accurate indicator of my faith, and I try to keep the total amount I give significantly above a ten-percent tithe.

I never give offerings based on my bills. In other words, I try to pray and give what I feel the Lord is directing me to give. When He shows me the amount, I give it without worrying whether that money should have been used for something else. If the Lord directs me to give money today that I was saving for a bill three days later, I always try to give today. Often I will consult with Kathy, and more often than not, she will confirm the exact amount I was considering to give. If she suggests an amount greater than I was anticipating, then I give that greater amount.

I stress that we give only after consulting the Lord and give the amount He directs us to give. It's irresponsible and presumptuous to blindly write checks for God's work when you have bills due. I've found that only on occasion has He directed me to give money "beyond my means"—money that was to have been used to pay something else. When He has so directed, He has also provided to cover the need created by that unusual offering. At the same time, I've never tried to keep something in the bank as a cushion against the unexpected when the Lord has directed to give that money away.

The writer of Ecclesiastes advised you to "cast your bread upon the waters, for after many days you will find it again" (Ecclesiastes 11:1). Cast your bread regularly and abundantly and watch for the return to come in due season. Your faith will be rewarded.

Whenever I've gotten discouraged over my finances, I've pressed into God's Word for comfort and encouragement. Over the years, the following have been my favorite verses where finances are concerned.

Let us not become weary in doing good, for at the proper time we will reap a harvest if we do not give up (Galatians 6:9).

You need to persevere so that when you have done the will of God, you will receive what he has promised. For in just a very little while, "He who is coming will come and will not delay. But my righteous one will live by faith. And if he shrinks back, I will not be pleased with him." But we are not of those who shrink back and are destroyed, but of those who believe and are saved (Hebrews 10:36-39).

Give, and it will be given to you. A good measure, pressed down, shaken together and running over, will be poured into your lap. For with the measure you use, it will be measured to you (Luke 6:38).

Remember this: Whoever sows sparingly will also reap sparingly, and whoever sows generously will also reap generously (2 Corinthians 9:6).

And my God will meet all your needs according to his glorious riches in Christ Jesus (Philippians 4:19).

Money is something that you handle almost every day. It's therefore a pertinent indicator of your faith and how you're putting it into action.

2. Your life's purpose and goals

Section One led you through a discussion and exercises to help you identify your life's purpose. Assuming that you can now summarize it in one sentence, what do you have faith to accomplish with that purpose? What goals have you set that will be accomplished only through God's power released by your faith?

To help you with this, why don't you think about what you would do if money and time weren't factors. Would you start a business? If you answer yes, then how much money would that business make in its first ten years? How many would you employ? How much money would you give to the Lord's work?

My own faith goals include plans to start a ministry called "Gold Mine Development Corporation." I want to see thousands released to function in their God-given purpose and then equipped and trained to be efficient and organized. From there, I want to see those same principles applied in several Third World nations for which I carry a concern (that will challenge me to weed out all my teachings that are "American-ized" and not related to true kingdom principles, a challenge I truly welcome).

I have goals for my ongoing education, the number of books I would like to write, and some "chaotic" situations to which I would like to bring order in my lifetime. I have no idea how some of these will come about, but faith doesn't require me to have all the answers before I plan or act.

I have written these goals out and review them regularly. Some of them are far from being a reality, but then so was my getting a pulpit at one time. God worked that out, and He will work these out as well. If they never come to pass, I plan on dying in faith, having seen them and welcomed them from afar.

3. Your Bible study

I've never been very keen on reading the Bible straight through. I've done it with some success, but I've had much greater success studying topics and individuals in an in-depth manner. I would like to suggest some faith studies that have added a great deal to my understanding and ability to apply my faith. After all, if faith requires action, then maybe your first action step should be to study faith (but remember, don't study just to learn; study so you can swing into action).

A. Read the four gospels and record in your journal everything Jesus said using the words *faith* and believe. Record your thoughts on these verses, and group them as they fit together. You may want to highlight those verses with one particular color in your study Bible. From there, you can do the same for Paul's epistles, John's epistles, and James' letter. A comprehensive understanding of faith will come only when you get a complete overview, not just singling out your favorite verses.

B. Do a complete study of Hebrews 11. Assign some of the names mentioned in that chapter some space in your time management notebook, and then study their lives in the Bible. Keep notes of what you discover on those pages. Study each one with a view toward answering why they qualified to be listed in Hebrews 11. Single out one or two who are particularly relevant to your life and calling, and make them the object of more intense, long-term study.

C. Based on these studies, what changes can you make in your life? Write down the thoughts you have from this and discuss them with your pastor, mentor, spouse, and children. Remember, faith leads to action, so study with an eye toward doing something.

As we close, be reminded that nothing is too difficult for God. He is in the business of doing the impossible. With that in mind, have faith! No matter how bleak it looks, God can come through with the unexpected and miraculous. So dream and plan accordingly. Put your hand in God's and hold on for the ride of your life. As you do, you'll join with the heroes of faith and earn your own place in the ongoing rendition of Hebrews 11, a chapter that is still being written for the people of God who have faith.

I hope by now that you are convinced there is gold in your life. Your purpose and the goals you set are of great worth, more valuable than any riches this life can offer. Consequently, your time should be invested in those things that are the most meaningful for you and that will yield the greatest return. To avoid wasting time, you should organize your world so that you can give yourself to the highest priority at any given time.

Yet as I've stressed again and again, it's all for naught if you don't have faith, for "without faith it is impossible to please God" (Hebrews 11:6). Trust God for great things, just as the apostles did in Acts 6. Opportunities abound for those who walk in purpose and faith. May the Lord bless you on your faith journey, and may you hear those wonderful words, "Well done, good and faithful servant" at the end of the road.

Notes

Introduction

1   Richard Nelson Bolles, *The 1994 What Color is Your Parachute?* (Ten Speed Press, 1994), page 435.
2   Stephen R. Covey, *The 7 Habits of Highly Effective People* (New York: Simon & Shuster Inc., 1989), page 60.
3   Ibid., page 60.
4   Ibid., page 34.
5   Bolles, *The 1994 What Color is Your Parachute?*, page 435.
6   Ibid., page 447.

Section One
Effectiveness: Know Where to Stake Your Claim

1   Covey, *The 7 Habits*, page 98.
2   Peter Drucker, *The Effective Executive* (New York: Harper & Row, 1966), pages 52,70.
3   Covey, *The 7 Habits*, page 71.
4   Ibid, page 128.
5   Ibid, page 93.
6   Bolles, *The 1994 What Color is Your Parachute?*, page 438.
7   Christian History, Issue 31, page 3.
8   Christian History, Issue 31, page 34.
9   Christian History, Issue 31, page 4.
10 Bolles, *The 1994 What Color is Your Parachute?*, page 436.

Section Two
Excellence: Be Careful Where You Dig

1   Covey, *The 7 Habits*, page 43.
2   David Collins, *Man's Slave Becomes God's Scientist: George Washington Carver* (Milford, Michigan: Mott Media, 1981), pages 105-106.
3   *Remarks by Paul H. O'Neill*, Alcoa Organizational Meeting, August 9, 1991.
4   Covey, *The 7 Habits*, page 71.
5   Ibid, page 123.
6   Robert Schuller, *Tough-Minded Faith for Tender-Hearted People*

(Toronto: Bantam Books, 1983), page 110.

[7] Ibid., page 109.

Section Three
Efficiency: Don't Settle for Fool's Gold

[1] *Bits and Pieces*, April 1, 1993, page 7.
[2] *Christian History*, Issue 29, Volume X, No. 1, pages 2-3.
[3] Covey, *The 7 Habits*, pages 153-154.
[4] Wilbur Moorehead Smith, *The Biblical Doctrine of Heaven* (Chicago: Moody Press, 1968), page 192.
[5] Alec MacKenzie, *The Time Trap* (New York: American Management Association, 1990), page 3.
[6] Ibid., page 12.
[7] Ibid., page 43.
[8] Ibid., page 74.
[9] Covey, *The 7 Habits*, page 169.
[10] MacKenzie, *The Time Trap*, page 10.
[11] Covey, *The 7 Habits*, page 161.

Section Four
Organization: How To Stay on Top of Your "Lode"

[1] Stephanie Winston, *The Organized Executive* (New York: Warner Books, 1993), pages 19-20.
[2] Ibid., pages 20-21.
[3] MacKenzie, *The Time Trap*, page 111.

Section Five
"I'm Just an Old Chunk of Coal, But I'm Gonna Be a Diamond Someday

[1] Covey, *The 7 Habits*, page 98.
[2] Ibid, page 23.
[3] Ibid, page 28.
[4] Covey speaks of the principle that "all things are created twice." There's a mental or first creation, and a physical or second creation to all things (page 99). He then uses the construction of a home as an example. First the architect and builder create the house in every detail before anything is

started by the construction crew. While this may be true concerning some things, it cannot be applied to spiritual things. Noah's mind did not create the concept or reality of rain or the ark. Instead Noah's mind was the vessel God used to reveal and carry out His plans to build an ark.

[5] Covey, *The 7 Habits*, page 103.

GOLD MINE DEVELOPMENT CO.
Developing the gold in every individual

Dr. John W. Stanko, Author & President
P.O. Box 91069 • Pittsburgh, PA 15221-7069
412-242-4448 • Fax: 412-242-6506
E-mail: johnstanko@purposequest.com
www.purposequest.com

Gold Mine Development Company's mission is to conduct seminars, produce publications, and provide other resources that will help you and/or your company identify your purpose, set appropriate goals, and order your life to accomplish what you were created to do. GMDC offers the following services:
- Motivational speaking
- Time management seminars
- Leadership coaching
- Life purpose seminars
- Staff profiling and evaluation
- Natural Church Development™ profiles
- Conference and event coordination

OTHER BOOKS BY DR. STANKO:
I Wrote This Book on Purpose
In a humorous, penetrating style, John Stanko helps you sort through your life and determine what God's purpose is for you.   ISBN 1-58169-011-8   128 pg. PB $7.95

A Daily Dose of Proverbs
Here's a devotional that makes Proverbs come alive. With wit, humor, and candor, John Stanko illuminates the wisdom of Proverbs in the context of today's needs.
ISBN# 0-9637311-8-1   376 pg. PB $14.95

So Many Leaders…So Little Leadership
By combining the latest in leadership techniques with a solid biblical foundation, Dr. Stanko delivers cutting-edge tools for leaders.   ISBN# 1-58169-048-7   160 pg. PB $9.95